REF
ML
3929
.G66
1998

W9-AVG-174

R0127583397

Deep down in music : the art of the

Deep Down in Music

Deep Down

in Music

The Art of the Great Jazz Bassists

by Leslie Gourse

Foreword by Ron Carter

The Art of Jazz

FRANKLIN WATTS • A Division of Grolier Publishing
New York • London • Hong Kong • Sydney • Danbury, Connecticut

I am very grateful to E. Russell Primm III, editorial director of Franklin Watts, for his personal vision that helped me produce this book and others in this history of jazz series.

Special thanks also go to bassist, composer, and teacher Rufus Reid for his painstaking, invaluable fact checking, which extended to the spirit of some of the material. Thanks to bassists and professors Cecil McBee and Richard Davis for their advice and cooperation. And thanks to Kyle Hernandez for giving me access to his research project on jazz bassists.

Visit Franklin Watts on the Internet at: http://publishing.grolier.com

Cover and chapter art by Robert Hanewich
Interior art by Rosanne Kakos-Main
Photographs ©: AP/Wide World Photos: 115; Archive Photos: 71 (Bill Spilka); Archive Photos/Metronome Collection: 43, 52, 59, 81, 84; Florence and Carol Reiff/Corbis-Bettmann: 83 right; Frank Driggs Collection: 23, 28, 33, 40, 80, 82; Magnum Photos: 87 top, 92 (Guy Le Querrec); Michael Ochs Archives: 87 bottom, 88 (Tom Copi), 75, 104; Retna Ltd.: 68 (Veryl Oakland), 89, 124 (David Redfern), 63, 83 bottom (David Redfern/Redferns), 85 (Judi Schiller); Tom Copi: 86.

Library of Congress Cataloging-in-Publication Data
Gourse, Leslie.
Deep down in music: the art of the great jazz bassists / by Leslie Gourse.
p. cm. — (The art of jazz)
Includes bibliographical references, discography, and index.
Summary: Presents the lives and artistry of notable jazz bassists, traces their influence on one another, and investigates the impact of various innovations on the development of jazz music.

ISBN 0-531-11410-4(lib. bdg.)   0-531-15904-3 (pbk.)
1. Double-bassists–Biography–Juvenile literature. 2. Jazz musicians–Biography–Juvenile literature. 3. Jazz–History and criticism–Juvenile literature. [1. Musicians. 2. Jazz.]
I. Title. II. Series: Gourse, Leslie. Art of jazz.
ML3929.G66   1998
787.5'165'0922 — dc21
[B]   97–19903
                                                                 CIP
                                                                 AC MN

© 1998 Leslie Gourse
All rights reserved. Published simultaneously in Canada
Printed in the United States of America
1 2 3 4 5 6 7 8 9 0 R 07 06 05 04 03 02 01 00 99 98

REFERENCE
R01275 83397
MUSIC INFORMATION CENTER
VISUAL & PERFORMING ARTS
CHICAGO PUBLIC LIBRARY

Contents

Foreword

Here is the first book on jazz bass by bassists themselves, who "tell all" through a knowledgeable intermediary, author Leslie Gourse. With the help of thoughtful questions, Ms. Gourse has elicited and reported some of the inner thoughts of these masters on the whys and hows and whos of their chosen instrument.

Deep Down in Music includes the compelling voices of several important bassists, ranging from the young Christian McBride and Peter Washington to the venerable Milt Hinton. In some cases, when the subjects of her investigation have passed away—for example, Pops Foster, Charles Mingus, Jimmy Blanton—Ms. Gourse asks the surviving experts for their comments on the influence these players have had on the music and the development of acoustic bass, on other players, and on themselves. Her easygoing approach, her reputation as a writer (author of the book *Louis' Children* and numerous articles for *Frets* magazine, *Jazz Times*, *Bass Player* magazine, and *Jazz Educators Journal*), her long experience as a listener in nightclubs, and her concern for accuracy have led these musicians to make statements and answer questions with honesty and openness.

Deep Down in Music makes fascinating reading for musicians and non-musicians alike. I would like to think that it will do for the history of the jazz bass what the amplifier does for the modern jazz bassist.

Ron Carter

Ron Carter, with more than 2,000 recordings to his credit, is one of jazz's most original, prolific, and influential bassists. He performed with the acclaimed Miles Davis Quintet from 1963 to 1968, earned Grammy awards in 1988 and 1993, and is currently a Distinguished Professor of Music at the City College of New York. He has been named a 1998 American Jazz Master by the National Endowment for the Arts, one of the most prestigious jazz honors in the United States.

THE GREAT INNOVATORS ON BASS

on Carter, a master of modern bass playing ever since he joined a Miles Davis group in the 1960s, draws big crowds whenever he leads his own groups in clubs and concerts. In the jazz world, bassists who lead their own groups are rare. The word bass means "bottom." The bass, which plays the bottom note of the chords in songs to create the bass line, functions primarily as a supporting instrument for groups.

Robert Hurst, a successful young bassist, says, "Part of the mindset of being a bass player . . . is [to] get off on making other people sound good. It's like Magic Johnson [a legendary basketball player] making the assist instead of shooting the basket."[1]

One of the words used to describe the instrument—*contrabass*—is the name of the lowest octave on the piano. The register is so low that it takes a while for audiences to perceive the notes played there. It's easier to hear instruments with higher-pitched voices. So bassists have rarely had much glamour.

In the early days of the century, only bassists with the strongest sounds could make themselves heard when they plucked the strings of their huge, quiet-voiced instrument. By the late 1920s, electronic inventions began to enhance the sound of the bass well. Now amplifiers have become so sophisticated that a bass can be heard in a big concert hall, and the sound of the amplified instrument is almost as natural as when it is played without any amplification.

Techniques for playing the bass have developed enormously during the twentieth century, too—in part because amplifiers have allowed bassists the freedom to experiment. Bassists don't have to concentrate primarily on making themselves heard. Now they play not only the bottom line—the root notes of the chords—for groups; they solo, too. And bass players have become adept at soloing in the upper as well as the lower registers of their instrument. Jay Leonhart even sings his own lyrics while accompanying himself on bass. Usually his songs are witty, touching stories about the human condition. Though he doesn't concentrate on virtuoso playing, he often gets the loudest applause when he takes part in concerts, because he communicates well with audiences. He has found a way to solo and support the songs simultaneously.

Some bassists play such high notes that the bass sounds at times nearly like a guitar. Alex Blake, a modern bassist who works in a group that plays exotic Middle Eastern music, has even emulated the sound of the oud, a Middle Eastern string instrument. He plays at breakneck speed high on the bass's fingerboard.

Bassists have come a long way since the early days of the century, when musicians started to develop jazz. At that time, bassists had a limited role in groups. Some simply played a thumping, steady rhythm. Others played the bottom notes of the chords. Often the bassists were mainly comedians who spun their basses. The visual effect was beautiful because basses were often painted in bright colors.

Basses have a bridge—a separate piece of wood held in place by the strings—in the middle of the instrument. The more the bridge sticks out from the instrument, the farther the strings are elevated over the fingerboard. The more elevated they are, the more they can vibrate and the louder their sound. Early bassists slapped and snapped the elevated strings for a percussive sound, so they were called slap bassists. Early jazz groups usually used the tuba, also called the brass bass, to play the bottom notes of the chords for groups. The tuba could make louder sounds than the string bass.

But the tuba was a slow-moving instrument. It took a great deal of time and wind for a player to get from note to note. As jazz tempos became faster, groups needed an instrument that could play the bass line and keep up with other instruments. The bass was ideal, especially when amplification became possible. Then, because of the efforts, ideas, and dexterity of a handful of innovative string bassists and also because of the vision of group leaders who hired them, the string bass came to play more of an important harmonic, melodic, rhythmic, and timekeeping role in jazz. String bassists replaced tubists in jazz by the 1930s.

Jazz bassists play pizzicato; that is, they pull the strings of their instruments. Some people say they pluck the strings, but plucking is less forceful than the technique actually used by bassists. They pull the bass back toward them and the strings forward, creating great tension. It's as if an archer were launching an arrow from a bow. In this case, the bow is the bass, and the arrow is the sound of the note. Playing pizzicato is an important technique in jazz, because it enables players to define the rhythm clearly. Before jazz bassists began playing pizzicato, most played arco, which means they drew a bow across the strings. Arco originated as a technique for classical music. Today, jazz bassists use both techniques to play the bottom of the music, keep the time, and solo.

Drummers, who used to be the primary timekeepers, have developed into soloists whose timekeeping duties are sometimes secondary to their expression of creative, explosive, rhythmic ideas. And bassists can be responsible for keeping time for an entire group. When the size of a group is restricted, a bassist may be used instead of a drummer. The strength of a drummerless group emanates from the mysterious, pulsating, occasionally percussive sound of the bass. A group without a bass often sounds lost. Musicians can stray from a sense of cohesiveness if they don't have a bassist with them, just as a flock of sheep wanders if it doesn't have a collie to act as a shepherd and keep stragglers moving along.

The bass has several names; acoustic bass, contrabass, double bass, string bass, bass fiddle, and bass violin are the most common. With the left hand, a bassist fingers the notes on the fingerboard and, with the right hand, arcos and plucks the strings. As technology developed in the twentieth century, the bass guitar, or electric bass, became a force in jazz and pop music. All acoustic basses and some electric basses are unfretted instruments. Frets are lateral ridges placed across the fingerboard of string instruments such as the guitar, the banjo, and the mandolin—instruments usually not used in classical music. Frets guide a player's fingering of the notes. Without the visual guideposts of frets on the acoustic bass's fingerboard to mark where the notes are, a player must memorize those positions. Players have to learn them so thoroughly that they become a habit.

Just carrying a big string bass around is difficult. Bassists tour all over the world with expensive, antique instruments—usually made of spruce wood on the front and back, and maple on the sides holding the front and back plates together. The fingerboard on the front plate is usually ebony, the hardest wood in the world; the second-best choice is rosewood. Ebony can stand up to the greatest beating. That's especially important now that bass strings are made of steel rather than catgut. And basses are delicate. They can get cracked by bumps and jolts or altered and damaged by weather.

On bandstands, bassists get very little rest. Like drummers, they play all the time. And in part because of the instrument's low voice, which people have at times found amusing, bassists have found themselves the butt of jokes. In self-defense, they like to tell bass jokes themselves. The jokes reveal that many bassists are especially intelligent, patient people.

One joke is about a bassist whose father falls into a coma. His family stays by his side in the hospital and tries to wake him. The doctors try everything. But nothing works. The bassist, who is very devoted to his father, becomes worried because he's been at his father's side day after day and hasn't been practicing. So he brings his bass to the hospital room and starts playing. His father sits up and starts talking! Everyone is amazed. The bassist, though, just sighs and says, "That's normal. Everyone talks during the bass solo."

The Earliest Bassists

Even the joke signals the great distance that modern bassists have put between themselves and the pioneering days of jazz. There were no bass solos when bassists first joined jazz groups. The best bassists played a "thump-thump" sound for the walking bass line, combining the rhythm and the root note of the chords of songs.

The best-known early bassists began playing in New Orleans. Among the handful remembered by name are Bill Johnson, Pops Foster, Steve Brown, John Lindsay, and Wellman Braud. Some bassists probably played in other cities, but they did not make recordings. New Orleans bassists ensured their place in history by recording with jazz groups in the 1920s.

The earliest known jazz bassist was Bill Johnson, an African-American, who played in New Orleans until about 1908. He traveled to California to play for a while and then headed to Chicago, where he founded his own band. It was taken over by a New Orleans cornetist, Joe "King" Oliver. Johnson continued to play in King Oliver's band. But in 1923, when Johnson recorded with the band, he played the bass line on a banjo, because recording equipment still wasn't sophisticated enough to pick up the sound of the bass well. In 1928, when Johnson recorded for the Victor company with New Orleans-born clarinetist Johnny Dodds as group leader, Johnson did use his string bass. Microphones had improved enough to pick up the sound of his bass.

Steve Brown, a white bassist from New Orleans, heard the African-American string bassists and imitated them when he played in a group called the New Orleans Rhythm Kings. He went on to play with Jean Goldkette's well-known swing-era band, then moved along to work for Paul Whiteman, a famous dance-band leader. In the 1920s and 1930s, Brown was considered a good, swinging player. He kept the time with his reliable, thumping, walking bass style. Another white bassist from New Orleans was Chink Martin, who made a career in the 1920s. Like most bassists of the day, he also played tuba.

George Murphy "Pops" Foster found work in some of the best New Orleans bands in the second decade of the twentieth century. Then he went up the Mississippi River, playing in Fate Marable's steamboat band. Marable's groups helped spread the sound of jazz to the Midwest and the North. Of all these early jazz bass players, Foster is best known to students of jazz bass history because he made the most recordings, and many were done with famous jazz musicians. In the 1920s, having moved from New Orleans to California, he recorded with Oran "Hot Lips" Page, a good early jazz trumpeter and group leader. Then Pops worked with trumpeter Louis Armstrong, regarded as the father of modern jazz. Pops recorded with Armstrong in 1936. He also recorded with Fats Waller and performed (or "gigged," as jazz musicians say) with Duke Ellington.

The Revolutionary Jimmy Blanton

Ellington was the first important jazz musician to recognize the possibilities of the bass as an instrument for solos. He always featured a bass, even in the days when everybody else used a tuba. Most tubists played bass as their second instrument. In the late 1920s, Duke used New Orleans bassist Wellman Braud in the band. By the late 1930s, another bassist, Billy Taylor Sr. (who is no relation to a famous modern pianist by the same name), played with Duke.

Then along came Jimmy Blanton, who revolutionized early jazz bass techniques. Blanton had been influenced by Pops Foster, Wellman Braud, and other pioneers. Previous to Blanton, in most groups the tuba players had played the bass line with single blasts of tonality. When the bass started replacing the tuba, Blanton came to imagine that he could go beyond the usual walking bass technique. He used more tonalities and scales from the chords than previous bass players had done. He was the first to play the bass with long, flowing lines in the manner of a horn player. Ellington was delighted when he heard Blanton's ideas and abilities. A famous Ellington band recording of the song "Ko Ko" done in March 1940 features a Blanton bass solo.

Every bass player who heard Blanton appreciated his strength, creativity, vitality, and swing—his good beat. Altogether his playing was a taste of

14

honey, of good things to come. Blanton became a role model for every youngster aspiring to play bass and improvise on the instrument. To this day, bassists listen to Blanton's 1940 and 1941 recordings for inspiration and instruction. His achievement is particularly amazing because he died of tuberculosis in 1942, when he was in his early twenties.

Swing-Era Bassists
With and Without Classical Training

Jazz bassists taught themselves to play by ear in the early days. Most couldn't read music. By the 1930s, though, some began to have classical training. Milt Hinton, who joined Cab Calloway's popular band in the 1930s and toured the country, took classical violin lessons in Chicago in the 1920s. He switched to bass and tuba when he became aware of the greater commercial demand for those instruments in his world—a world in which African-Americans weren't welcome in the classical music field. He studied bass with a classical teacher, too.

John Kirby played the string bass with a respected swing-era band led by Fletcher Henderson in the 1930s. With Count Basie, Walter Page had a smeary, bluesy sound perfect for Basie's blues-based band. Page played with his thumb wrapped around the neck of the bass and slid his hands up and down the fingerboard, playing by ear and by instinct.

Whether classically trained or self-taught, these early jazz bassists were inspired by their predecessors, the pioneers who played pizzicato in Pops Foster's generation. Pizzicato playing was the great innovation for jazz bass techniques. Gradually the slap bass style became old-fashioned. It passed out of jazz almost entirely by 1940.

Occasionally a modern player still slaps the bass, but only for dramatic, percussive, and rhythmic effect and "to have a good time and remember the good old days," as modern player Cecil McBee says.[2] McBee began playing clarinet in the 1950s and then acoustic bass in his native Oklahoma. As a teenager, he heard a few older musicians playing slap bass. Alex Blake, who emulates the sound of the Middle Eastern oud, slaps the bass's strings for an exciting, percussive effect.

Oscar Pettiford in Bebop Groups

In the 1940s, along came a bassist named Oscar Pettiford, with "a big, hairy beat," as many people have described his powerful rhythmic gift and his sound, which is loud even without electronic amplifiers. He began exploring modern harmonies with the beboppers—a group of revolutionary jazz musicians in the 1940s in New York. Pettiford has inspired most bassists since those days. Like Blanton, Pettiford is considered a major innovator of bass techniques. After Blanton died at a young age, Pettiford extended Blanton's ideas, playing longer and more creative solos.

Advances in Fingering

Through tours and recordings, American jazz musicians impressed Europeans so much that some musicians in Europe abandoned classical careers and concentrated on playing jazz. Many European jazz musicians became very fine players, but few exerted a major influence on the styles of Americans. An exception is a Danish jazz lover, Niels-Henning Orsted Pedersen, who began playing pizzicato with three fingers, not just one, the way most Americans did. When American jazz bassists heard his remarkable speed, powerful sound, and beautiful, emotionally transporting, fluid lines, they started to practice and streamline their own technique. Now all modern bassists play with several fingers; the number they use at any one time depends on what they are playing.

Electronics and the Flowering of the Acoustic Bass

Electronics enhance the dynamics—the loudness or quietness of a sound. The quality of the pure, acoustic sound can be lost through electronics, too. But engineers kept improving amplification technology throughout the twentieth century. Now amplifiers are so refined that they rarely change or compromise the beauty of the acoustic bass's natural sound.

There have been notable bass players throughout the history of jazz. But especially when playing techniques and electronic equipment made it easier for bassists to make themselves heard, more youngsters, who loved the deep voice of the bass, wanted to play it. Since the 1950s, there has been a flowering of talented jazz bassists. Several have become group leaders.

Charles Mingus, one of the most important composers in jazz, played bass. In the 1950s, he led his groups in startling directions with his compositions and his ideas about improvisatory playing. Some people argue that Mingus was not one of the best bass players, but actually he was one of the most important composers, leaders, improvisers, and innovators in the history of jazz and the bass. And his personal, often radically wild, inspirational style served his purposes so well that he ranks as one of the greatest artists on jazz bass.

Mingus belonged to a generation that nourished diversity in jazz. There were, among the most influential stylists on all the instruments, modal players, who used a series of notes rather than chords as their inspiration for improvisation. Then the avant garde—free jazz players—started using the outer extensions of chords to compose or improvise. Or they used no chords at all. People had become used to hearing the basic three-tone triad—the root note plus the 3rd and 5th intervals of a chord. The innovators in the late 1950s played music based on the 7th, 9th, 11th, and 13th tones of the chord, which add color to the chords. Solos didn't have to retain any chordal center, progressions, or forms except for the inventions in the imaginations of the players. Gone was the twelve-bar blues form; the thirty-two-bar American popular song disappeared from free jazz, too. The structure of songs was longer and looser. Sometimes players substituted cacophony. And sometimes, as in Mingus's music, beautiful melodies and cacophony blended for emotional excitement.

The virtuosity of other players, both sidemen and leaders, could lift ordinary groups to the level of the legendary. Bassist Leroy Vinnegar, who began playing at the end of the swing era, had a particularly strong, walking bass line style, which inspired young bassists who heard his recordings. "Slam" Stewart played with the great pianist Art Tatum after becoming very popular in a group with pianist Slim Gaillard.

A very swinging musician, Stewart was well known for singing in unison with his bass playing. He amplified his own sound without the help of electronic devices, achieving an otherworldly sound—an echo—by singing the exact same note that he was playing with his bow on the strings. His main protégé was a bassist named Major Holley. Holley had such a deep voice that he could sing along in the bass register with his instrument. The combination heightened the effect of his unison singing to the maximum degree.

Ray Brown Sr. began his career with Dizzy Gillespie's band in the late 1940s and became one of the greatest bassists in the history of the art. A creative, supportive player and an incredible soloist, he imbibed the influence of Blanton and Pettiford, synthesized it, and went his own way, becoming more agile and harmonically brilliant.

Another of the most remarkable bass players is Ron Carter, a classically trained musician and teacher, who became prominent in a group led by trumpeter Miles Davis in the 1960s. Miles, a modal player, required improvisation from his sidemen as part of the foundation of his group's sound. Most bass players since then have aspired to play with the virtuosity, power, and musical understanding that Carter exudes.

Electric Basses

In the 1960s and 1970s, electric basses became popular in rock music and fusion jazz. Jaco Pastorius, a great technician who played emotionally stirring music on his instrument, blazed trails. Some electric bass players would eventually have custom-designed instruments with six strings instead of the original four. They wanted the extra strings to take advantage of the instrument's ability to play higher and lower tones.

A British pop singer and electric bass player, Sting, became a superstar—a rarity in the bass-playing world. In the jazz world, where the acoustic bass remains king, electric bass player Bob Cranshaw is revered for his command of the instrument, and he is welcomed in acoustic groups. And many electric bass players, such as James Jamerson, who played for Motown recording sessions, influenced other electric players in the jazz and pop music worlds. This book concentrates on the acoustic players because they are the primary movers for traditional jazz.

The Acoustic Bass Moves Center Stage— Sometimes

A poignancy remains about the destiny of the acoustic bass players. Despite the advances in technology that allow their instruments to be heard playing anything the bassists dare to attempt, the bass is still a low-voiced, background instrument. Acoustic bassists must build momentum slowly and surely and dazzle audiences at the same time. A bass player aspiring to become a popular leader must transcend, with showmanship, spirit, and technique, the primary role of the bass.

To this day, unless a bassist leads a group, he or she is hired to play the foundation of the music first and foremost. If a bassist can solo, too, that's fine. But the bassist must be able to play supportively. Even if a bassist leads a group, he or she must still support all the instrumentalists and make the sound and ideas emanate from the bass. Like the hub of a wheel, the bassist should hold all the other instrumentalists in a group together. And they extend the work of the bassist-leader to present a total performance.

It seems as if there are limitless challenges for bassists. They must find ways to cover the big intervals, or physical distances, between notes. They must play in tune and with perfect time and have a good beat, which means they must maintain the time and play it with great spirit and excitement. Even if they stand out front as leaders, they never emit the clarion call of a trumpeter. They can never steal the thunder through sheer loudness. They must struggle to make their instruments sparkle in solos in a low register.

Bassists have taken giant steps throughout the twentieth century. Through the force of their virtuosity, swinging feeling, harmonic and melodic brilliance, and showmanship, players such as Milt Hinton (eighty-seven years old in 1997), Ray Brown, Ron Carter, Cecil McBee, and younger bassists Rufus Reid, Ray Drummond, Avery Sharpe, and Christian McBride (age twenty-five in 1997) can attract all the attention in a group. Canny leaders sometimes set Ray Drummond center stage, because audiences love to hear his daring, flowing, fleet lines and watch his head bob from side to side as he becomes carried away with his impassioned music. Ron Carter plays gorgeous melodies on the piccolo bass, a slightly smaller, higher-voiced bass, in his own groups. In the hands of great modern players, who can execute virtually any idea they can dream up, the deep, intimate sound of the bass can beckon like a voice from beyond and hold audiences rapt.

2

POPS FOSTER AND THE SLAP BASSISTS OF NEW ORLEANS

Whenever anyone speaks of the earliest bassists in jazz, Pops Foster's name comes up right away. He was a forceful character with a swinging bass-playing style to match. He said there was nothing he liked better than "romping" on an uptempo song and slapping out a good rhythm.[1]

Born on May 19, 1892, on the McCall Plantation in Louisiana, about 60 miles (90 km) from New Orleans, George Murphy "Pops" Foster grew up among share-cropping African-Americans. They grew sugarcane and corn. His father, Charlie Foster, worked as a butler at the plantation house and could speak French. But in plain English, Pops said he thought his father was "no good."[2] He spent his money on liquor, put himself in debt to the company store, and never brought anything home to his kids.

His wife, Annie, and the children ate food from "the pan"—the left-overs, often very good food, from the plantation house meals. (The pan was a Louisiana custom.) Pops said his mother sewed, knitted, and crocheted to help make ends meet.

Pops's older brother, Willie, a violinist, made a primitive bass out of wood and twine for Pops to play when he was still a little boy. He had to climb up on a stool to reach the top of the fingerboard. His first jobs were playing in the Foster Family band.

His father was so abusive that his mother fled the countryside with her sons and daughter to live with a relative in New Orleans. Pops, who was ten at the time, felt as if he had suddenly been transplanted from the nineteenth to the twentieth century. Everywhere Pops looked, he saw places for musicians to work. On Sunday afternoons, he went to Lincoln Park, where he was fascinated by bassist Henry Kimball, who played in the John Robichaux band, a well-known New Orleans group. Admission into the show area was fifteen cents. Pops was lucky if he had a nickel for the street-car to get home, so he used to sneak into the show. A policeman once asked him what he was doing. Pops said he was watching the bassist. The policeman suggested he learn to play the bass, too. He said, "That's what I'm trying to do."[3]

His father tried to get the family together again, but Annie refused. Pops was so angry at his father for beating up the family that he threatened to kill him. His father died—of either tuberculosis or cancer—in 1906. Pops never mentioned feeling any sense of loss at his father's death. Instead the boy enjoyed his life with his mother, brother, and sister. He didn't do well in school because he was always busy listening to music or playing music at night. So he slept through his classes and dropped out of school in the fifth grade. Later he would tell everyone to stay in school because he regretted not getting an education.

But when he was a boy, school did not seem to him to be the road to opportunity. In New Orleans, music was played in public every day. He became friendly with all the New Orleans musicians—a bassist named Jim Johnson, for one. All the musicians in town formed a small segment of New Orleans's African-American society by themselves.

Pops Foster and the Slap Bassists

By 1906, when he was fourteen, Pops got a job playing in the Rozelle Band, which had been started by his brother, Willie, and other musicians. Pops also played with little groups for lawn parties and fish fries. That's when Willie bought Pops a real bass.

In those days, musicians always had day jobs to make ends meet. Pops became a longshoreman. Such hard physical labor may have helped him develop the great strength and stamina he needed to play his instrument and make it heard in the midst of all the other, naturally louder instruments.

Pops played for dances and parties in dairies and honky-tonks—any-place that needed a band. At lawn parties, the organizers cooked catfish and gumbo and prepared ham sandwiches, potato salad, and ice cream. "A plate of gumbo was fifteen cents," he recalled. "It usually cost twenty-five cents to get in [to the party] and it was a good way to make a little change. Around Chicago and New York they had the same thing, but they called them 'house rent parties.' . . . String trios would get a whole lot of jobs around New Orleans where they wanted soft music. . . . It was a lot more pleasure for me to play in the string trios than in the brass bands."[4] At the dairy dances, which ended when the cows started mooing to be milked, he earned seventy-five cents to $1.25 to play for the night. "Sometimes we'd be romping real good and keep playing with the mooing going on," he recalled.[5]

In 1908, Pops moved on to the Magnolia band, led by Louis Keppard, the brother of famous New Orleans cornetist Freddie Keppard. Joe "King" Oliver, a cornetist who would lead a popular band in Chicago in the 1920s, played in the Magnolia band, too. The Magnolia was one of the best-paid bands in Storyville, the red-light district of New Orleans. There, legal and illegal entertainment was exciting, swinging, and a bit dangerous, filled with hustlers, prostitutes, gamblers, and all sorts of slick people who earned their livings by their wits. Fights often broke out. But Pops enjoyed the lifestyle among professional musicians there and worked proudly in New Orleans bands into the 1920s.

"We had plenty of fun together and there was music everywhere. If the rest of the world was like musicians, this world would be a great world," he later wrote in his autobiography.[6]

*P*ops Foster, 1934

Pops met Bill Johnson, the older bass player who became a friend and left town when Pops was just a boy. In New Orleans's tight-knit society of musicians, Johnson and an early jazz pianist, Jelly Roll Morton, were friends and brothers-in-law.

Pops played with many musicians who have become known as pioneers of jazz in New Orleans in the first and second decades of the twentieth century. He remembered when Storyville was shut down by the U.S. Department of the Navy on November 12, 1917. Jazz had become synonymous with vice in the district. The closing of Storyville plus the rise of the swing-band era gave jazz a better image, Pops thought. After Storyville was closed, he played elsewhere in town. He also worked in Fate Marable's band on the Mississippi riverboats.

By 1922, like many New Orleans musicians, Pops left town for good in search of work. That year, he recorded with a band led by Oran "Hot Lips" Page in California. Pops made connections with other popular musicians in the swing era. He played with bandleader Horace Henderson, pianists Jelly Roll Morton and Willie "the Lion" Smith, and even with Duke Ellington in 1931.

Pops devised his own technique. In classical technique, the bass is angled or leaned toward a player so he can get the left hand completely around the fingerboard. And a classical player uses a bow drawn across the strings. Pops was a two-fisted, rough-and-ready player who picked the strings forcefully in the pizzicato style. He raised the strings very high up over the bridge in the middle of the bass, so that when he slapped them, he got the percussive, snapping sound so essential to producing a definitive rhythmic foundation—the forward momentum and swing of jazz. He slapped the fingerboard with the open palm of the right hand while grasping the strings to be plucked. And he held the bass upright and kept his elbow lowered. He had enough physical strength to dominate the sound. Slapping was considered a hot sound, like the growl of the trumpet or the trombone. But more important for a jazz group was a bassist's ability to swing by playing in the pizzicato style. Pops was one of the first to use this new technique.

Telling about his early influences, aside from the early bass players he heard, Pops said, "I used to pick up ideas from everybody. Sometimes I would find an alley guitar player, playing only blues, and give him a quarter to play all those pretty chords they used to go through."[7]

He made his first recording in St. Louis for the Okeh label in 1924, with Charlie Creath's Jazzomaniacs. But recording techniques weren't very good at the time. Pops's best recordings would be done just after World War II, in the late 1940s, even though by then a more modern, melodic style of bass playing had been developed. But he always enjoyed his role as a slap bassist: "I don't like to play solos," he wrote.[8]

Though he worked and recorded with some of the best early jazz and swing-era musicians, his musical career had terrific financial ups and downs. By 1942, when he was living in New York, he found so little work that he took a job as a porter in the subway system. The pay was very low, but his bosses let him sneak away from work and take music jobs whenever they came up.

Pops kept romping—swinging—whenever he could. It was during the times when he had trouble earning a living that he realized he should have stayed in school. Education might have made his life easier, he came to understand. But no matter how difficult life sometimes was for Pops financially, he always had the respect of other jazz musicians because of his strength and swing.

In 1946 or 1947, hanging out in a legendary New York jazz club called Jimmy Ryan's, he told other musicians, "Hell, I just play any old go-to-hell note as long as it swings!" Bassist Bill Crow heard that remark at a time in his career when he was struggling to get the notes right. Much later on, when he matured into a fine, contemporary player, he realized what Pops was saying: "If the notes a musician plays add to the feeling of swinging together with the rest of the group, then they're probably the right ones. . . . [Guitarist] Jim Hall and [pianist] Hank Jones . . . will take any old go-to-hell note one might play and make it sound like a brilliant and gorgeous choice by surrounding it with a heavenly chord."[9]

By any standards, Pops Foster was an exciting player, though he remained a slap bassist—a primitive, pioneering player—all his life. "His rhythm was so sure and firm that he was really better to work with than most young, technically advanced bassists," said Vince Guaraldi, a San Francisco pianist who played with Pops late in his career.[10]

Pops could sing in a trio and bow the bass part at the same time, as he did in September 1963 as part of an Earl Hines group. Hines, an innovator of modern jazz piano, was making a comeback in the jazz world. Bowing was an important part of Pops's style. He bowed first, then picked, adding to the rhythmic crescendo that was traditionally an important element in classic jazz. His arco sound was big and gritty, not a pretty, singing, bel canto sound, and equal to any recorded bassist before Jimmy Blanton. Using his bow the way a violinist did, Pops showed the effect of his brother Willie's lessons.

Most early bassists actually played in a very rudimentary way with the bow, and Pops was no exception. But he also understood harmony, and he knew about technical, classical concepts for bass players. He wanted to put a bass quartet together in the 1950s, at a time when it was a very farfetched, progressive idea.

There were few fast players among the early bassists. But Pops played a more modern-sounding, four-beat style while others in New Orleans were playing two beats (they all played in 4/4 time, but early jazz, or Dixieland, had the feel of 2/4 time because of syncopation that emphasized the weak beats in the measure.)For his time, he was very trendy and accomplished. Bandleaders were glad to have him for their rhythmic foundation. Luis Russell, a Panamanian who grew up in New Orleans and led a highly respected band in the swing era, kept Pops as a player from 1929 to 1937. With Louis Armstrong in 1936, Pops had a big, chomping sound. He always got a big hand from audiences.

George Duvivier, a great self-taught modern jazz bassist who had started with classical training on the violin, would always remember the day he discovered the great chasm between himself and Pops. Duvivier's generation of bassists came to take amplification and musical education for granted. George was playing with a group one day in New York when Pops Foster came into the club. Out of courtesy, musicians often invite guests to sit in, so Pops went onto the bandstand, and he played Duvivier's bass with such strength that he pulled the bridge to one side. Duvivier's heart was in his mouth; luckily, Pops did no lasting damage to the bass.

Rudi Blesh, whose book *Shining Trumpets* extols the early jazz musicians, said, "Pops may not have done 180 miles an hour on the super highway. He just laid out the highway, that's all."[11] He was, in any case, the one who got the most credit. In middle age, he moved to San Francisco, where he found work and respect as a bassist, though his slap bass style had long since become outdated. He died in October 1969, from heart failure and other illnesses.

Other Early Bassists

Among the other important bass players from New Orleans was *Bill Johnson.* Born in Talladega, Alabama, in the early 1870s, he played bass and tuba in brass bands and was in the Eagle Band in New Orleans by 1902.

In about 1908, Johnson traveled across the Southwest to Los Angeles in a band sometimes called the Original Creole Band. When the group disbanded in 1918, Johnson moved to Chicago, started a band, and turned it over to Joe "King" Oliver at Lincoln Gardens in 1922 to go freelance. In 1924, recording with Louis Armstrong, Johnson played the bass line on the banjo, because recording techniques weren't good enough yet to pick up the sound of the string bass. A driving slap bassist, Johnson recorded with the bass in Johnny Dodds's Washboard Band in 1926 for the Victor company. By then, the art of electronics had become sophisticated enough to catch the sound of the instrument. He stopped playing in the 1950s, undoubtedly slowed down by his age, and retired to Texas.

Although legend credits younger men with inventing the pizzicato style of playing jazz bass, Bill Johnson was probably already playing that way before Pops Foster and his generation did. Everyone was influenced by Johnson and probably by Henry Kimball, too. Kimball was the bassist in the John Robichaux band who had fascinated young Pops Foster in New Orleans.

Born on January 13, 1890, in New Orleans, *Steve Brown*, a white bass player who began on tuba, worked in a family band, then moved to Chicago in 1915. There he made a recording with the New Orleans Rhythm Kings in 1922. Between 1924 and 1928 he played with Jean Goldkette's orchestra, then Paul Whiteman's band, two famous dance

*B*ill Johnson was the bassist in Joe "King" Oliver's band in the 1920s; Oliver is standing beside him. Seated in the center is Louis Armstrong.

bands of the early swing era. On his recordings with Goldkette, Brown showed off his great ability to swing.

An African-American cornet player, Rex Stewart, who played with Duke Ellington and also wrote about jazz, recalled the day he first heard Goldkette's band in New York's Roseland Ballroom in 1927. He wrote that the band "hit Roseland . . . like a tempestuous, tropical storm. . . . We in the Fletcher Henderson Band were amazed, angry, morose and bewildered as we sat on the opposite bandstand waiting our turn to go on." Henderson's band, which usually got respectful treatment, had to wait longer than usual because the audience kept cheering for Goldkette. "In our hearts, we knew . . . we simply could not compete with Jean Goldkette's Victor Recording Orchestra. Their arrangements were too imaginative and their rhythm too strong, what with Steve Brown slapping hell out of that bass fiddle and Frankie Trumbauer's inspiring leadership as he stood in front wailing on his C-melody saxophone."[12] He added, "Brown brought the art of slapping the bass fiddle direct from New Orleans, where he had heard the Negroes do it."[13]

The Goldkette band folded in 1927 because of an inflated payroll and poor booking prospects. Then Paul Whiteman took Steve Brown and other popular Goldkette veterans into his band. Brown's swinging, old-fashioned approach ranged from playing two-to-the-bar patterns (a standard rhythmic effect) to contrapuntal triplets and clever, off-the-beat accents. Brown eventually moved on to Detroit, where he freelanced in the 1930s and 1940s as a player and bandleader. He died there in 1965.

John Lindsay, an African-American musician born in New Orleans on August 23, 1894, started playing the bass as a teenager and went on to play trombone, working with some of the same bands as Pops Foster in the early 1920s. Then Lindsay worked on the riverboats, recorded in New York, and settled in Chicago by 1925. He switched back to bass, toured with Louis Armstrong's big band in 1931 and 1932, and appeared with Armstrong in a short film, *Rhapsody in Black and Blue*.

Lindsay worked with Jimmie Noone and Johnny Dodds, both clarinetists who led their own bands. Noone was born in New Orleans and migrated to Chicago. During the swing era, his band, broadcasting live on radio shows called "remotes" from the Apex Club in Chicago, attracted many fans.

Lindsay played on classic early jazz recordings with Jelly Roll Morton's Red Hot Peppers band in Chicago in 1926. He both plucked and slapped the bass in the traditional, entertaining, rhythmic style of the day.

Another early bass and tuba player, **Billy Taylor Sr.**, was born in Washington, D.C., on April 3, 1906. Moving to New York at age eighteen, he played with several well-known bands, most notably Duke Ellington's in the 1920s. He recorded with McKinney's Cotton Pickers in 1929 and toured with that group for a year. In 1934, he performed with the great Harlem piano player and composer Fats Waller, then with Fletcher Henderson's band. Henderson's arrangements inspired all the bands, regardless of the race of their leaders and instrumentalists.

Taylor worked again with Duke Ellington from 1935 to 1940. The Ellington connection boosted his career more. He recorded with other sidemen in Ellington's band, including clarinetist Barney Bigard, trumpeter Cootie Williams, and legendary alto saxophonist Johnny Hodges. In the 1940s, Taylor had many other illustrious jobs in jazz, including work with Coleman Hawkins, a major stylist for tenor saxophone.

Wellman Braud, who was born in St. James Parish, Louisiana, on January 25, 1891, played various string instruments in New Orleans. He also played drums in brass bands. By 1917, he settled in Chicago, where he started playing bass with various bands. In 1923, he toured Europe with Will Vodery's Plantation Revue. (Vodery was an important arranger who supplied the jazz feeling for the Ziegfeld Follies, the vaudeville show in New York City in the 1920s.)

In 1927, working in New York City, Braud joined Duke Ellington's band and played with it until 1935. He was active with some of the best, most imaginative musicians of the day, playing and recording with Louisiana-born artists Jelly Roll Morton, soprano saxophonist Sidney Bechet, and cornetist Bunk Johnson. Braud also worked with a very zany scat singer, Leo Watson, whose group was called The Spirits of Rhythm. Watson made up wild lyrics to embellish songs; he did a weird tune about snakes, for example, calling out, "Snakes snakes cobras boa constrictors Baaaaaaaaaah lalalalalalalla . . . wah wah woooo."[14]

Braud claimed to have developed the concept of the walking bass—that technique, so important to jazz, of plucking the bass strings and playing the root of the chords to combine rhythm and harmony. He valued the big tone that he produced from slapping the strings against the fingerboard—the slap bass technique—even though he knew he overdid it. He called it "overplaying."[15]

These were the pioneers and adventurers for early bass playing. Compact discs of bands led by Jelly Roll Morton, Fats Waller, Louis Armstrong, and Duke Ellington reveal how the bassists sounded in the 1920s and 1930s. Every big band had a bassist playing pretty much the same way by the 1930s.

3

JIMMY BLANTON IN THE DUKE ELLINGTON BAND

The slap bassists had to work so hard to make themselves heard that they really never had the luxury of refining their art. By the late 1920s, recording techniques began to improve. It would be another two decades before amps and pickups helped the bass be heard even more.

The amp (amplifier) takes its signal from the pickup—an acoustic-electrical device that converts the vibrations of the bass's strings into electrical impulses—and enlarges and enhances the sound, which is heard through the loudspeaker system. That system converts the electrical impulses, which have been fed by the pickup to the amplifier, back to sound. The microphone does the same thing for any instrument or voice. In the days when whole bands used one microphone, the sound of the bass was drowned out. So sound engineers felt motivated to develop pickups for the bass.

The bassist Jimmy Blanton was born at the right moment—October 1918—as recording techniques were beginning to improve the bass sound. And he had the talent to use the improvements in electronics to produce artistic, refined music.

He was a formidable addition to Ellington's rhythm section. The orchestra's recordings suddenly sounded more swinging and modern. The reason was Blanton's great vitality, swing, harmonic sophistication, and melodic, hornlike lines. At Ellington's urging, Blanton began soloing on the bass. His choice of notes and his good beat—the spirit with which he played, blending rhythm and harmony—alerted the jazz world.

Every bassist who came after Blanton listened to his recordings with Duke for inspiration and guidance. No longer was the bassist confined to playing the traditional walking bass part. Blanton's ideas helped lead to the development of the rhythm section composed of piano, bass, and drum and paved the way for the expanded role the bass would have in bebop in the 1940s.

Blanton was born in Chattanooga, Tennessee, into a musical family. His uncle taught music theory; his mother was a pianist. Jimmy learned from the melodic lines she played. He started playing violin, then switched to three-string bass at Tennessee State College. In the summers he worked in Fate Marable's band on the Mississippi riverboats. In the late 1930s, he moved to St. Louis, Missouri, where he found jobs playing the bass professionally with a band called the Jeter-Pillars Orchestra.

In 1939, he was playing in an after-hours joint in St. Louis. Duke Ellington's band, touring the country, was in town, playing at the Coronado Hotel. One night, after the Ellington band finished its job, arranger Billy Strayhorn and saxophonist Ben Webster headed to the "hot spot," as Duke called the place where Blanton was playing.[1] Duke's men had never heard of Blanton, but they were charmed by his strong sound and musical sophistication. He knew the chords so well that he

Jimmy Blanton at the Savoy Ballroom in New York City in 1940

could play exactly the right notes for the foundation of the music. His beat and his feeling inspired Duke's men, too. Soon Duke went to hear Blanton and talked him into playing a few songs with the band at the Coronado. Then Duke hired him on the spot.

Duke encouraged Blanton to play solos; they weren't very long, but they were harmonically and melodically beautiful. He used both the bow and the pizzicato technique with ease. He supplied everything that a band could need for support. He played round, full tones precisely in tune and with a propelling sense of swing. He went beyond the strict quarter note accompaniment of other bassists of his era, playing eighth and sixteenth notes for a more modern, intense sound in the ensemble parts.

In the space of about two years, he made more than 130 recordings with Duke's band, plus some recordings with small groups of Duke's sidemen. He even recorded in a duo with Duke himself. The big-band era was in full swing. Dance bands crisscrossed the country and broadcast from hotel ballrooms. Every band had a bassist, and every bassist paid attention to Jimmy Blanton's innovations. Blanton's resonance on such masterpieces as "Ko Ko" and "Concerto for Cootie" (which became popular with lyrics as "Do Nothing 'til You Hear From Me") helped make Duke's orchestra a superior group.

Bassist Billy Taylor Sr. was playing for Duke when Blanton came into the band. For a while, both bassists continued to work, but Blanton was getting all the attention and praise. He was featured on one tune called "Jack the Bear," which audiences called for time and again. His special friend in the band, tenor saxophonist Ben Webster, nicknamed Blanton "Bear." Duke featured Blanton on other tunes, too, including "Plucked Again" and "Pitter Panther Patter." One night, when the band was playing in the Southland Café in Boston, Billy Taylor picked up his bass in the middle of the set, packed it up, and quit. He told Duke, "I'm not going to stand up here next to that young boy playing all that bass and be embarrassed." Duke hated to see the talented older bassist go, but facts were facts.[2]

Ben Webster was Blanton's opposite in personality. Blanton didn't smoke, drink, or gamble, and he saved his money. His buddy Ben loved to drink, and he was always getting into scrapes. One night, bassist Milt Hinton, who played in Cab Calloway's band, asked Ben to repay a loan. Ben showed up on a street corner to pay the debt. Blanton was with him. Ben, who had no money, said, "Bear, you got any money?" Hinton recalled, "Blanton reached into his watch pocket and pulled out a roll of fifty-dollar bills. He peeled off four and gave them to me."[3]

Hinton also remembered that Blanton, who was physically weak, walked out of a club into the chilly night air, still drenched with sweat after performing all night. Sometimes Blanton got on a bus soaking wet after a gig and traveled "two or three hundred miles while his clothes dried on him," Hinton said.[4] By late 1941, Blanton was feeling sick, but he kept touring with Duke's band.

He loved playing so much that, after working for a night with Duke, he sometimes got together with other musicians and went out on the scene to jam until morning. In the early 1940s, a group of pioneers in jazz—Dizzy Gillespie, Charlie Parker, Thelonious Monk, and their followers—began developing progressive jazz at Minton's Playhouse in Harlem. Blanton sometimes went there. Not only bassists but the horn players, pianists, drummers, and everyone else paid attention to Blanton's style.

In Los Angeles, Blanton and drummer Lee Young used to make the rounds of clubs to jam for free with Nat "King" Cole. Cole was still a struggling pianist and trio leader in small clubs for a few dollars a night. Red Callender, a young bassist who had moved to California, idolized Blanton: "I used to carry my bass around for him to play it. Take him all over town. He'd never sleep. I'd sit up and listen to him play all night."[5]

Blanton didn't complain about not feeling well. One legend says he told his roommate in Duke's band that he was leaving the band for a little while to visit someone in his family. But Duke found out that Blanton was sick and took him to a sanitarium. Blanton had tuberculosis. There was no penicillin or sulphur drugs at the time, and tuberculosis was a leading killer.

Deep Down in Music

Duke's band was leaving Los Angeles after a gig in 1942. Ben Webster asked Milt Hinton to keep an eye on Blanton—Calloway's band was playing next at the same ballroom. "He's pretty sick," Ben said. "Go out to see him." Hinton hired a car and went every other day to the sanitarium outside of town.[6] Blanton was only twenty-two; far from his Tennessee home, he didn't have a close friend or relative in California. Hinton thought Blanton seemed very lonely, even brokenhearted to be so sick in a strange city. He thought Blanton was getting weaker, losing his will to live.

There's another legend that someone took Blanton out of the sanitarium to a neighboring state and put him in a dirty place where he had no decent medical care. When Duke found out, he moved Blanton back to the sanitarium in California. In either case, Blanton died there in July 1942.

Musicians kept listening to his recordings. After Blanton, the most important innovator for the jazz bass style was Oscar Pettiford, who was born on an Indian reservation in Oklahoma. With his family, he moved to Minneapolis, where he was living in 1939, the year that Blanton joined Duke's band. Oscar heard Blanton play that year, possibly in Minneapolis. "When I heard him, I was in love with him right away. I was just with him one night. We had a head-cutting contest [a playing competition] right away. Our approaches were a lot alike. We hung out from early evening to break of day," Oscar told the jazz writer Nat Hentoff during an interview in 1957.[7] When Blanton died, Pettiford felt that it was his responsibility to keep developing the bass and finish the amazing work that Blanton had begun.

4

MILT HILTON
AND OTHER
BIG-BAND
BASSISTS

Once the bassists played pizzicato and developed a horn-like conception for playing solos, the jazz bass style became more elaborate.

Bassists still thought their primary job was to support the entire group. Milt Hinton has said, "The bass is a service instrument. The word base [of which "bass" is a variation] means support, foundation. If you put up a building, the foundation must be steady and strong. I must identify the chord for everyone, and only after that can I play the other notes. You learn to have a lot of humility. You must be content in the background, knowing you're holding the whole thing together."[1]

One and all, the musicians who became bass players have said they were attracted to the low sound of the instrument. Most of them knew they would probably never command the attention accorded the trumpeters, the pianists, and the saxophone players. Bass players made their peace with their position in the background. A few with strong instincts to lead groups made special efforts to do so. Often they felt frustrated because it was difficult to convince club owners and recording company executives to give bass players the chance to take center stage.

John Kirby, who was born in Baltimore, Maryland, on December 31, 1908, was one of the few bassists to lead a band in the swing era. Between 1930 and 1935, Kirby went back and forth from the bands of Fletcher Henderson and drummer Chick Webb, until, in 1937, he took his own trio into the Onyx Club on West 52nd Street in New York. The street had so many little jazz clubs featuring so many stars that it became known as Swing Street. Kirby was successful enough (though not considered a great bass player) that the following year he was able to book a sextet with his wife, the fine singer Maxine Sullivan, in other jazz clubs.

Kirby's group was very popular. It played in clubs, broadcast on radio, and made records with a nationwide following. His musicians played sophisticated arrangements, many of them written by the group's exceptionally gifted trumpeter, Charlie Shavers. Saxophonist Russell Procope, who also played with Duke Ellington's band, and Billy Kyle, a pianist for Louis Armstrong, worked in Kirby's sextet. They played in a softly stated but firm swing-era style.

During World War II, the band kept losing its members to the draft. By 1946, it had broken up, a casualty of the war, financial pressures, and the changing fashions in popular music. By 1948, almost all the big bands had broken up because leaders could not afford to move them around the country. Also during the war, people became more attracted to small combos, with their soft, intimate sounds propelled by a rhythm section of piano, bass, and guitar, than to the big bands.

In Kansas City, *Walter Page*, a bass player born in Missouri in 1900, worked with pianist Bennie Moten's band, then started his own group, the Blue Devils, in Oklahoma. Many famous African-

American players, among them Count Basie, worked in Page's band. By 1931, the Page band folded. Page began playing in Count Basie's band, called the Barons of Rhythm. It was booked to play jazz in the Reno Club in Kansas City in 1936. That year, talent scouts for New York recording and booking agencies heard the band broadcast live on shortwave radio and rushed to Kansas City to sign Basie to contracts. At the end of the 1930s, the band became famous for its versions of "One O'Clock Jump" and "Jumpin' at the Woodside," among other songs. Jimmy Rushing, a short, fat, charming entertainer, sang the blues for Basie.

Basie, Page, and drummer "Papa" Jo Jones were called the All-American Rhythm Section. As so many bassists did, Page freed the left hand of the pianist. Basie had been steeped in stride, in which the left hand played a striding rhythm. Page, with his self-taught, smeary style perfect for Basie's blues-based band, took over that rhythm, freeing Basie to concentrate on harmonies. And with his talent as a timekeeper, Page also freed the drummer, Jo Jones, a former dancer, to become more creative and play the pulse of the music on the hi-hat cymbals. Jones's revolutionary concept set a new standard for a lighter, dancing sound for modern drummers.

Page is just one example of the impact of big-band bassists on the development of jazz. George T. Simon writes in *The Big Band Era*, an authoritative book on the period, that when *Metronome* magazine asked readers to choose their favorite swing bands, they chose about three hundred bands. There were hundreds more in the country—some with national reputations, others playing only in certain regions. Each band had a bassist.

But bassists were rarely even mentioned in Simon's book or other histories of the era. Among the few who received notice were Jimmy Blanton, Steve Brown, Bill Johnson, John Kirby, Walter Page, Israel Crosby, Oscar Pettiford, Ray Brown, Slam Stewart, Al Hall, and Milt Hinton. Left out were such important players as George Duvivier, one of the most accomplished bassists of the late swing and bebop eras and throughout all of modern jazz history. In the late 1930s, Duvivier

W alter Page

played at Kelly's Stable on Swing Street with Coleman Hawkins, who defined the jazz style for the tenor saxophone. By the 1950s, Duvivier was a familiar figure on the studio recording scene in New York City.

Of the bassists who began their careers, or even worked for their entire lives, in the big bands, few ever became famous. But their work steadily contributed to the emergence of the bass as a force in modern jazz. Milt Hinton, who by 1995 was nearly the only surviving bassist of prominence to have begun his career in the 1920s, recorded their influence in his autobiography, *Bass Line*. It preserves forever the flavor of the era in which he and the art of playing jazz on the bass matured.

Milt Hinton

In *Bass Line*, one of the best and most humane and flowing stories about any portion of jazz history, Milt Hinton tells of living in a shack on stilts in Vicksburg, Mississippi, where he was born in 1910, and witnessing a lynching by a crazy mob. When he was nine years old, he and his family took a horse and carriage to the railroad station. The segregated coach for African-Americans on the train carrying them north "smelled like rotten food and it was noisy," he wrote.[2] Perhaps the last thing in the world that one might have dreamed of for Milt Hinton's future was an illustrious career as a musician and a photographer, but that is precisely what he achieved.

Though his mother wanted him to play the piano, Milt chose the violin. Slowly he progressed until he could quit his newspaper delivery route and earn money regularly as a musician. His tales about his family life, including his own job as an illegal moonshine deliverer for the mob run by gangster Al Capone during Prohibition, make for exciting reading. Milt was thrilled with the interesting, soulful music he heard on Chicago's South Side, the African-American neighborhood where he lived.

A short child who wore glasses, he had to figure out ways to escape from the bullies in school. He had a breezy, friendly way of dealing with people. And his musical talent qualified him for the All City Orchestra, made up of the best musicians from both African-American and white high schools in Chicago. "Most kids had to wait until they were seniors to get in, but I made it for three years straight. . . . Actually the first two years I played violin, but by the third year I'd made the switch over to bass."[3]

Chicago, then with the biggest African-American community in the northern United States, had many clubs, theaters, ballrooms, and private societies. Musicians played in all of them. Milt heard Duke Ellington's band and admired Duke's bassist, Wellman Braud, a "dignified New Orleans gentleman."[4] He always hoped that Braud would talk to him. Braud was polite and smiled and said hello, but he never started a conversation with the young hopeful.

Milt switched to bass when the introduction of movies with sound-tracks changed the entertainment industry. After the Al Jolson movie *The Jazz Singer* in 1927, audiences clamored for "talkies"—movies with sound and music in them. Musicians, many violinists among them, lost their jobs in the movie houses.

Around that time, a miracle happened to Milt. A businessman who was an amateur bassist took eight high school bass players to his down-town department store and showed them a room full of basses. "Okay, try them out," he told the kids. After a while, he asked them if they had found basses they liked. Milt had picked one. "The bass you picked is yours for as long as you play bass. If you ever decide to give up playing, bring it back to where you got it," the man said.[5]

Milt was still playing the same bass in the 1990s. It was a Tyrolean three-quarter bass viola that had been made in Germany in the late eighteenth century. When Milt came to own several basses, he loaned them to other struggling musicians so that they could earn money and buy basses of their own. He never sold a bass, because he regarded bass playing as the saving grace of his life.

An only child, he was encouraged to play music by one of his aunts and his grandmother. He struggled to get along with his mother. "To be honest, I had a young mother who acted more like a bossy older sister than anything else. . . . [S]he never seemed to spend a lot of time with

M ilt Hinton

me. . . . She had such a short temper. . . . I don't ever remember a time when my mother took me in her arms and made me feel like I was her darling. Mama [his grandmother] was the one who did that. . . . She was my guiding angel and she showed me she loved me in all kinds of ways.

"Music came to mean more to me than anything else. I started playing the violin at thirteen and from that point on, whenever something had happened, I'd go off alone and play music. It became my religion. It was my salvation and it sustained me.

"I was very young when I decided that as long as I treated music well, it had to do the same thing for me. I knew I'd never give it up no matter what the hardships. And I never did."[6]

He started college, but he was working as a musician at night and sleeping through his classes. His teacher found out Milt was earning one hundred dollars a week as a musician—more than most people were earning at any job during the Depression. The teacher told Milt to quit college, keep working, and concentrate on studying music. Milt kept playing with all the local heroes on the Chicago scene and the nationally prominent jazz stars who passed through town. And he had the thrill of his life when he began working for his idol, Eddie South, a great jazz violinist, and traveling with South's group to California. In 1933, Milt had the chance to play at the World's Fair. At the time, he recalled, the walking bass style had not yet become popular.

"In fact, bass playing seemed to evolve pretty slowly. In my opinion . . . it was because the bass players around had switched from tuba and didn't know much about the techniques of playing string instruments. So at first the bass was given a percussive role, the same way tuba was used. Musically, it was kept simple. Everyone played the major note in a chord, period. Most things, including stock arrangements, were played in two-beat [that is, syncopated]. So, for example, if you had an F chord, you'd play two F's to the bar. But sometimes on the last chorus the band might get hot and then you'd play four beats of the same note.

"I'd taken harmony courses at [college] so I knew something about chord structures, but nobody had taught me anything about using music theory in a practical way." He experimented with playing a chord himself the way everyone else did, then becoming increasingly daring. He began "playing the one and five notes in a chord. So if I had an F chord I'd play F and C instead of all F's. Then a little later I began using other notes in the chord, too.

"I figured out that my instrument had to identify a chord, so I'd always play the tonic [the lowest, root note of the chord] as the first note. But I also realized that after the tonic I could play a lot of other notes in the chord. So for example, if I had an F chord I'd play an F first, and follow it with an A and a C, and then maybe go to a D and put in the sixth. From a harmonic standpoint there are many acceptable notes, but I began to get a feeling for what combination sounded best, especially when I made the transition from one chord to the next. I was walking, but it took a long time before things flowed naturally. . . . [T]here were a lot of other bass players experimenting during this time. I'm not saying I was the originator, but I know I was one of the contributors."[7] He was playing the root notes of the chords but also improvising other notes in the chord that enhanced the music for the entire group.

He did his share of slap bass playing. But instead of doing single slaps, the way Johnson, Braud, Brown, and Foster had done, he went on to double and even triple slaps. "I also worked out a way to put the bass between my legs while I was playing and I'd ride it like a horse across the stage," he said.[8]

Popular bandleader Cab Calloway, passing through Chicago, hired Hinton to take the place of a handsome bassist, Al Morgan, who went to work in the movies in Hollywood. Hinton stayed with Cab from 1936 until the band broke up in 1951.

Hinton's account of his first night with Calloway's band is hilarious. He was wearing Al Morgan's old uniform, which was too big for him. Milt was wearing his hair in a trendy pompadour style with a great deal of pomade holding a big wave in place over his forehead. And he was set down in front of the band. "The whole band hit and I really got shook. I'd never been put out in front of a band that large with such a strong brass section. When all those horns suddenly came in, I thought the wind was going to blow me over." There were no parts written out for him. So he watched the left hand of the piano player, who called out the keys and the more difficult chord changes to him. After four or five songs, Milt was swinging, he thought.

Then Cab called out "Reefer Man," one of his hit tunes. The song was supposed to feature the bassist, but Hinton didn't know that. The piano player told him, "It starts in F. When he stomps off, you grab F and you keep playin' an F chord. It's yours alone until he brings the band in." Milt recalled, "I grabbed F, I squared F, I cubed F, I chromaticized F. I was scared to death and I was playing way over my head. I was fast—lightning fast."

He did so well that the men in the band called to him to keep going. His clothes became drenched with sweat. His pomade melted; his hair stood straight up on his head. Cab let him play alone for about five minutes before he called the rest of the band in. To Milt, it seemed as if he had played for an hour. At the end of the song, the bass player was supposed to act as if he were overcome and fall back into the pianist's arms. Hinton did it. He passed the test.[9]

With the Calloway band, Milt had one of the best jobs in music—one hundred dollars a week to start and paid vacations at Christmastime. For six months of the year, the band worked in the Cotton Club in Harlem. Hinton recorded and played in little groups with some of the best swing-era musicians in all of jazz. The rest of the year the men toured, with all the hardships that entailed, made far worse by racial prejudice in the South. Sometimes living conditions in the North were pretty bad, too.

As he traveled, Hinton began taking photographs. Throughout the years, he would take at least forty thousand artistic photos recording the experiences of jazz musicians on the road. Eventually the pictures were mounted in highly-praised shows around the world. In the band, Ben Webster, the tenor saxophonist, influenced the flow of Milt's music—the way Milt went from chord to chord. Trumpeter Dizzy Gillespie, who joined the band in 1939, used to take Milt to the roof of the Cotton Club to rehearse. Dizzy was trying to modernize Milt's way of walking the chords. Dizzy analyzed the songs Milt played and got him to play flatted fifths and other modern note substitutions. Milt didn't always understand what Dizzy was doing. Dizzy demonstrated by playing the bass line on his trumpet. Dizzy was busy igniting a musical revolution, creating a more intense, fiery, complex style of jazz called bebop.

To keep himself fresh while he was playing the same music year after year for Cab, Milt played unfamiliar music for himself all the time. He worked with a bow, trying to get his sound right. He read every piece of music that came before his eyes, just for the practice. He studied with a man named Dmitri Shmuklovsky, who played with the Chicago Civic Opera and had a reputation as a fine teacher. At first Shmuklovsky didn't want to teach a popular band player, but Milt convinced him that he wanted to know everything about playing the instrument. Shmuklovsky gave Hinton a finishing course in bass playing.

Milt did so well in the Calloway band that he and his wife, Mona, bought a house in Queens, New York. By the late 1940s, though, the band business began to die out. Cab broke up his band and worked with smaller groups that included Milt. Milt was fired and rehired often, depending on whether Cab could find bookings. He had to take any job he could, including one at a dive on the New Jersey waterfront for very low pay.

He bumped into comedian Jackie Gleason on the street one day. They had hung out together on the road during the days when Gleason was struggling. Gleason found out that Hinton had fallen on hard times and hired him to play for an album he was recording the next day for Capitol Records. It was called *Music for Lovers Only*. It became very popular and gave Milt's studio career a boost.

There had always been prejudice against African-American players in the studios; the assumption was that they couldn't read music. When Milt showed up to play for Gleason's record date, a white bassist was sitting in the studio; in fact, Milt was the only African-American musician there that day. The white bassist was given the parts that had to be played with a bow, and Milt was asked to play pizzicato. He had a beautiful bass with him, and that helped break the ice between the white players and him. Trumpet player Bobby Hackett, an old friend of Milt's, was in the studio and greeted him warmly. That, too, helped put everyone at ease. Milt was invited to come back the next day.

From then on, Milt's life became crammed with bookings. He played in the most prominent clubs and the best recording studios, where the pay was excellent. His strong, rich sound and perfect timing didn't decline an iota as he grew older. If anything, his sound grew burnished.

For his eighty-fifth birthday, he gave a concert to raise money for a scholarship in the name of bassist Major Holley. At the concert in the New School's auditorium in New York's Greenwich Village, Milt sang lyrics and played one of his original songs from the album *Laughing at Life*. It was about how mean Father Time was, but Milt was still playing and laughing at life. The beat reverberated throughout the auditorium. Everyone could feel the pulse that radiated from the old master.

Other Big-Band Bassists

Al Hall, who was born in March 1915 in Jacksonville, Florida, grew up in Philadelphia, where he trained on the cello, tuba, and double bass, hoping for a career in symphonic music. He started to focus on the bass in 1932. Discovering that the classical orchestras had no openings for African-American musicians, he headed for the jazz scene in New York City. There he played at the Savoy Ballroom and eventually at Café Society Downtown, Manhattan's first racially integrated club, and its Upper East Side offshoot, the Blue Angel.

He also played and recorded with swing-era pianist Teddy Wilson beginning in 1938 and with other well-known pianists, including Ellis Larkins, Mary Lou Williams, and Clyde Hart. Bebop drummer Kenny Clarke worked with Hall, too. Hall started his own label, called Wax, and led groups on several recordings before selling Wax to Atlantic Records. From 1945 to 1963, Hall played with Erroll Garner, the stylish, rhythmically unique pianist and composer of the very popular song "Misty."

Hall also played with clarinetist Benny Goodman, guitarist Tiny Grimes, singer Alberta Hunter (who came out of retirement in her eighties to star at a club called the Cookery), and until Hall's death in 1988, trumpeter Doc Cheatham for Sunday brunches at Sweet Basil, a leading New York jazz club.

Al McGibbon, who was born in January 1919 in Chicago, in the center of a thriving blues and jazz scene, established himself in his twenties with leading jazz bands in New York City in the 1940s. For his full tone and steady beat, he was hired by bandleaders Lucky Millinder, J. C. Heard, and Coleman Hawkins. McGibbon was so adaptable that he could play with stride-based pianists Earl Hines and Count Basie as well as bebop innovator Thelonious Monk, whose music was distinguished by odd harmonies and hesitant rhythms. McGibbon also played with pianist George Shearing's group during Shearing's very popular Latin jazz period. All these diverse pianists had begun playing in the stride style, so McGibbon knew the roots of their music intimately.

Eddie Safransky, born on Christmas Day in 1918 in Pittsburgh, Pennsylvania, started as a violinist, then became a bassist in high school. By the end of the big-band era, he was playing with the bands of Miff Mole, Stan Kenton, and Charlie Barnet. Boosted especially by his playing in Kenton's band, for which Safransky swung with a steady beat and an articulate style, he eventually became a studio player and a staff musician with NBC.

These and many more big-band players went on to distinguish themselves in the jazz world, even as it went through many changes in the coming decades.

5

SLAM STEWART AND MAJOR HOLLEY

Many bassists who began their careers in bands went on to distinguish themselves in small groups. Some became composers, arrangers, or educators. Only two became well known for their unusual technique of singing in unison with their bass playing.

Slam Stewart

Leroy Elliott "Slam" Stewart, born on September 21, 1914, in Englewood, New Jersey, began playing the violin at an early age. He loved listening to the big bands on radio, especially Jimmy Lunceford's and Duke Ellington's. By chance, in his high school's music room, he discovered a bass fiddle that no one was using. "I had to have a young fiddler teach me to tune it," he recalled.[1] He taught himself to play, though he never learned the correct fingering. George Duvivier would say that it made his "hair stand on end" to see how Stewart, one of his idols, fingered the bass.[2] Nevertheless, few jazz bassists ever mastered the instrument as Slam did.

With his parents' encouragement, Stewart enrolled in the Boston Conservatory of Music in 1934. To help make ends meet, he played a few gigs. In one combo, he met an alto saxophonist, Ray Perry, who also played jazz on the violin and sang a few choruses in unison with it. "I was fascinated," Stewart recalled. "I thought: 'Why can't I do that on the bass fiddle?' But my voice wasn't low enough. So I changed my voice and sang an octave higher [than the bass's register], making sure that I kept my voice as close to the bass as possible. . . . I think the technique was Ray Perry's own little invention. He sang in the same register with the violin, that high register. As soon as I heard it, I wondered what he was trying to do. And I'm very thankful to him."[3]

Without enough money to stay at the conservatory for more than a year, he went to New York City, where he happened to visit a well-known Harlem club called Jock's Place. Slim Gaillard, pianist, singer, and composer of the popular novelty tunes "Flat Foot Floogey With the Floy Floy" and "Cement Mixer Puttee Puttee," was playing there. In time-tested jazz tradition, Stewart sat in with Slim. It just so happened that Gaillard had a program to do on WNEW radio the next day. He invited Stewart to play for the show. The duo was so appealing that Martin Block, a famous disc jockey, became their manager, booked them at many places, and arranged recording dates. Slam earned his nickname around that time by tapping the floor fairly hard with his foot while he played.

Slim and Slam became popular before World War II. In 1941, Slim went into the service. Slam went to work with other well-known group leaders. His recordings with pianist Art Tatum's trio are considered jazz classics. Not only could the peerless Tatum do no wrong—his hands were so fast and dexterous that audiences never knew which hand was playing what—but Stewart was a good, solid player who could use the bow exceptionally well.

Slam Stewart

The team of Slim and Slam never played together on a regular basis again. Slim Gaillard lived a disorganized life. He telephoned Slam from time to time. Sometimes the calls came from England, where Slim was passing through various hotels and leaving the rent unpaid. He always reversed the charges to Slam. But their original team had kicked off Slam's enduring, highly respected career, which encompassed about 350 record sides—mostly jazz recordings.

In 1968, Slam settled in Binghamton, New York, where he presented jazz workshops at a state university. His wife, a pianist, taught jazz history at public schools in the area. Slam stressed ear training for anybody who wanted to try his style of singing in unison with an instrument. "Learn the notes," he advised. "That's part of ear training. . . . Then add the heart."[4]

Major Holley

A few other musicians have tried unison singing very successfully. One is guitarist George Benson, who had many hits, such as "This Masquerade." But only one other bassist, Major Holley, made unison singing his specialty. Holley, too, bowed his solos instead of plucking them. Stewart's sound was melodious. Holley's was low and rumbling, and he often invented his own witty lyrics for his compositions.

He was born in Detroit, Michigan, on July 10, 1924, into a very musical family. At first, Holley played the violin. In navy bands during World War II, he played the bass and discovered that he preferred that instrument's low sound. He also wanted to play the foundation of the chords. Holley took advantage of the GI Bill of Rights to study music at a college in Minnesota. He also married a young woman, but she had a drinking problem and left him. In her early twenties, she died of complications from her alcoholism. The loss broke his heart. He left school and began working as a musician full-time.

He had already heard Slam Stewart playing and singing in unison on the tune "Champagne Lullaby" in 1938. "My first reaction," Holley recalled, "was to say 'What the hell is that?' I wasn't even playing the bass then. I didn't think that I would ever do it. But I had to find out what it was about."[5]

To sing in unison, Holley recommended that a musician first learn all the nuances and qualities of the bass. "Once you learn the bass, you're free. Then the voice must be on pitch. If a bassist sings exactly in tune with another sound, the sound is amplified."

Holley tuned his bass the standard way, from high to low, G-D-A-E, then sang along. "The secret is to sing in tune with what you play," he stressed. Unlike Slam, Holley had a very deep singing voice. Though he didn't have perfect pitch, he said, he soon learned that he had to blend his voice with that of the bass to get his reverberating sound. "If you draw the bow across the A string, you must be able to sing exactly what that string dictates," he explained.

Through the years, Holley had to fight some audience prejudice against his bass voice. "Not too many great bass parts were written for orchestras," he said. "Audiences prefer a high, falsetto man's voice to just an out-and-out bass singer. In the great operatic works, tenors and sopranos have the leads."

People sometimes considered singing in unison with the bass as buffoonery, he added. "A few people hate the sound of singing in unison to a bass. They don't understand it. If they knew how hard it was to do, they'd shut up about it. . . . It's like playing with a bow. A great and serious study."

With the eventual emergence of the electric bass, with its smaller intervals and its capacities for soloists, the acoustic bass was regarded as the rhythm instrument. "Now it has a complete legitimacy all its own," Holley said in 1983, reviewing his career and the development of techniques for playing the acoustic bass during his lifetime. "So young kids are coming out [of schools] with exact sciences."

A few younger bassists asked Holley to teach them to sing in unison. Several took lessons, but they gave up quickly, deciding to concentrate on instrumental techniques. One young bassist named Lyn Seaton persisted. By the 1980s, Lyn Seaton had learned his lessons well and was featured as a unison-singing bassist with many groups.

Slam Stewart died in December 1987. Soon afterward, Holley, who always said, "I'm standing in the shadow of Slam Stewart," and who had made duo albums with Slam, helped lead a memorial service at St. Peter's Lutheran Church in New York. Not enough people showed up to satisfy Holley. At a concert later that day, Holley got up onstage and scolded the audience for not showing up in massive numbers for the great Slam Stewart. He wound up his impassioned narration by saying, "Reverend Holley has spoken!"

Holley enjoyed a busy career, playing with stars from the swing and bebop eras, among them Dexter Gordon, Charlie Parker, Ella Fitzgerald, and Oscar Peterson. In the 1950s, he worked as a studio musician for BBC television in London. He toured South America with clarinetist Woody Herman's big band. Returning to the United States, he played with saxophonists Al Cohn and Zoot Sims.

In the 1960s, he became well known as a studio musician and kept performing with many famous group leaders, including guitarist Kenny Burrell, Coleman Hawkins, and Duke Ellington. He sang in unison with his bass on studio dates for Frank Sinatra, too; his reverberating sound delighted Sinatra.

Holley toured Europe with singer Helen Humes, who had begun her career with Count Basie's band. He recorded with saxophonist Lee Konitz, trumpeter Roy Eldridge, and pianist Sir Roland Hanna. He taught at the Berklee College of Music in Boston from 1967 to 1970. He often led his groups with young sidemen playing in duos and trios in New York jazz clubs. Audiences were lured to the clubs by Major's reputation.

During his last years, he toured constantly, hopping from Brazil to New York to Europe. Like most jazz musicians, he found he could earn more money if he toured the world and maintained an aura of glamour. In 1991, he felt sick with a stomach ache and cut short a tour in Germany. Resting at his girlfriend's house, he died of heart failure in his sleep. His memorial service at St. Peter's Church was crowded to the rafters.

INNOVATORS OF MODERN BASS— OSCAR PETTIFORD AND RAY BROWN

Oscar Pettiford

Techniques for playing the bass in jazz groups took another giant step forward when Oscar Pettiford came on the scene. He was a wild, mercurial man who had a weakness for alcohol. But his brightness as a bass player streaked like a meteor across the jazz world.

Oscar was born on an Indian reservation in Okmulgee, Oklahoma, on September 30, 1922, and moved with his musical family to Minneapolis when he was three. He started his career in his family's band. First he danced at age six, then he played piano, trombone, and trumpet. The trumpet hurt his jaws, he said, "and I studied tailoring in case the music business ever got tough."[1]

An older sister, a pianist and reed player, gave Oscar music lessons. In his early teens, he began playing bass. At age seventeen, in 1939, he heard Jimmy Blanton play with

Duke Ellington's band, probably in Minneapolis. After Blanton's death, Pettiford felt it was his responsibility to keep developing jazz bass—"to keep it moving," he told writer Nat Hentoff.[2] He wanted to emphasize the hornlike lines and embellish the usual techniques for playing the roots of the chords and keeping the beat. He wanted to play with greater complexity than other bassists, who used basic quarter notes even in solos.

Pettiford was also influenced by Minneapolis bassist Adolphus Alsbrook, who had played with both Duke Ellington and Count Basie, and by Milt Hinton, who passed through town with Cab Calloway's band. Pettiford also paid attention to Billy Taylor Sr., who had preceded Blanton in the Ellington band; to Mose Allen, who played with Jimmy Lunceford's band; and to Israel Crosby when he played with Fletcher Henderson in the early 1940s.

Milt Hinton was very impressed with Oscar's talent. When Pettiford stopped playing because gigs were so scarce in 1942, Hinton gave him pep talks. "Milt talked me back into music," Pettiford recalled. " 'Man,' he said, 'don't let talent go down the drain. There ain't nobody here playing like you. And you could more than hold your own in New York.' "[3]

From January to May 1943, he played in a two-bass team with Chubby Jackson, who was also in Barnet's band. He continued playing with other great musicians, too, and he "once carried his bass for two miles in sub-zero weather—without gloves—to make a jam session in a Chicago hotel with Charlie Parker and Dizzy Gillespie."[4]

Then Charlie Barnet, a white saxophonist who led racially mixed swing bands, passed through Minneapolis and hired Pettiford to go on the road in May 1943. Oscar's headquarters became New York City, where he found that nobody could outplay him.

In New York, Oscar made such a great impression that he was invited to play for his first recording in 1943 with the award winners in *Esquire* magazine's critics' poll. Then Oscar himself won the *Esquire* Gold Award in 1944 and 1945, a prestigious honor in the jazz world.

Pettiford followed the young beboppers to Minton's Playhouse in Harlem, where he worked with house pianist Thelonious Monk, who was called "the high priest of bebop." Monk was working on new harmonies and guiding Dizzy Gillespie in developing the new style. When Dizzy organized one of the first bebop groups to play on West 52nd Street, Oscar became his coleader. Oscar helped the beboppers arrange their material, suggesting that the horns in the front line play in unison, instead of one horn playing out front and the other playing accompaniment in the background. That unison playing was an important idea for bebop. Dizzy noted, "Oscar was a driving force in that music."[5] Pettiford contributed some lines to the beboppers' new compositions. His song "Bass Face" was the basis of "One Bass Hit," which the younger bassist Ray Brown recorded with Dizzy in 1946.

But Oscar's antics on and off the bandstand upset Dizzy. Oscar frequently quit the group. He was winning polls and had a great opinion of himself. Dizzy called him "a prima donna."[6] The group split up. After that, Oscar and Dizzy each led his own groups on 52nd Street.

In November 1945, Pettiford was invited to join the Duke Ellington band, a great honor. He stayed until March 1948. He had always wanted to play in Duke's band. Although some of his favorite players had left the band by the time he joined, he still managed to record some fascinating music with Ellington.

In 1948, he was leading a small group again, a trio at the Three Deuces on 52nd Street, first with the great piano player Erroll Garner and later with George Shearing. After that Pettiford took a big all-star band into a club called the Royal Roost. By 1949, Oscar was playing in Woody Herman's band. There he worked with wonderful players his own age, among them saxophonists Stan Getz and Zoot Sims and drummer Shelly Manne—all destined for fame.

Oscar saw a cello in a music store and was invited to try it. The fingering for cello is different, the positions are smaller, and the instrument is tuned differently, but Oscar magically began playing the cello well on the spot. He broke his arm soon afterward and had to stop playing everything for a while. But when he went back to work, touring with a group led by drummer Louis Bellson and trumpeter Charlie Shavers, he played both the bass and the cello regularly.

*O*scar Pettiford (left) in the recording studio with Billy Strayhorn, Duke Ellington (reclining), studio bassist Lloyd Trotman, and jazz writer and producer Leonard Feather.

He never learned to live in a regular way, however. In December 1950, he was given the honor of leading his own group of fine musicians on a USO tour through Asia and the Pacific Islands. By January 7, 1951, though, he was fired and sent back to the United States. He had gotten into a fight with his own guitarist. The guitarist told Army officials the fight was his fault, but actually, both men had been drinking and both were at fault. Pettiford was drinking heavily during the whole trip. "Oscar just drinks too much, he likes to socialize, and he has a terrible temper," said jazz writer Ralph Gleason.[7]

The fiasco did the image of jazz absolutely no good. But Oscar kept playing. From 1952 to 1958, he led his own groups in Café Bohemia, a popular jazz club in the heart of Greenwich Village. By that time, the 52nd Street clubs had closed. Café Bohemia's house band belonged to Pettiford, who played with authority and commanded the respect of his sidemen. Among his compositions, which he required the group to play, was "Bohemia After Dark."

Pianist Dick Katz was playing in Oscar's group at another club, Jazz City, in New York in the 1950s, when bassist Charles Mingus's group was on the same bill. Mingus and Pettiford alternated, introducing each other as "the world's greatest bass player." Katz recalled, "Pettiford had this amplifier, which he didn't need. It was tuned up so loud that it was louder than the horns. I couldn't hear what I was playing. 'I'm the leader, and I want to be heard,' he would say. I would sneak in and turn it down, and he'd turn it up. Someone else would turn it down, and he'd turn it up."[8]

To many people, Oscar seemed egomaniacal. But his playing, with his beat and great taste, did everything for the status of the bass. As a pizzicato player, he had no peer, so forceful was his sound emanating from a group.

Pettiford left the United States in 1958 to play in England with an all-star touring group called Jazz at Carnegie Hall. When the tour ended, he stayed in Europe to work. He was playing at an art exhibit in Copenhagen in September 1960 when he became ill. After a few days, he died in a hospital from a virus that started with a strep throat. His hard-drinking lifestyle, in addition to the rigors of the jazz world—the constant travel, the strange hotels, the bad food in many restaurants, the uncertainty of payments, the smoky jazz clubs in the wee hours of the mornings—contributed to his death a couple of weeks before his thirty-eighth birthday. But he had been driven to excel as a musician, and he set standards for bass players that lasted forever.

Ray Brown

The only other bass player in Pettiford's generation to become as influential was Ray Brown. Brown played superbly and was particularly fascinated with the foundation of the music. He also wrote a book, *Ray Brown Bass Method*, and became a venerated teacher. Born on October 13, 1926, Brown was still going strong as a group leader in 1997. The best young players wanted to work in his groups.

Both Pettiford and Brown were incredibly strong players. If Pettiford was perhaps more artistically driven, Brown might be considered the better man to fit in with a group and propel a rhythm section. He had a balanced approach to his instrument and personal life. And Brown has lived much longer than Pettiford, acquiring more experience and formal musical education. He constantly won awards from music magazine readers and critics as the top acoustic bassist.

For building a career, nothing is more helpful than good health and longevity, and of course, practice on the instrument. Brown recommended that bassists practice ten hours a day to become professionals and that they learn a great many tunes and play them in every key.

He praised Jimmy Blanton as his major influence, and he saw the melodic Oscar Pettiford and aggressive Slam Stewart as important influences on his style as well. Born in Pittsburgh, Pennsylvania, Brown found a bass to practice on in high school and loved its low voice. When he graduated, he was already earning money as a professional player.

On the road at age nineteen, he found himself in Florida, touring with Snookum Russell's band. He and two other players "began plotting to go to New York and try our luck," he recalled. "But the night before we were to go, everybody chickened out, leaving me with my bags all packed. So I said, 'The hell with it,' and went."[9]

He stayed in his aunt's apartment, and his nephew took him down to 52nd Street. That night, he saw many of his idols—singers Billie Holiday and Billy Daniels, tenor saxophonist Coleman Hawkins, and pianists Erroll Garner, Art Tatum, and Hank Jones. Ray had already met Hank. As they were talking, Hank told him that Dizzy Gillespie had just walked into the club. Hank introduced Ray to Dizzy, calling Ray a friend and a very good bass player.

Dizzy nearly gave Ray a heart attack by saying, "You want a gig? Be at my house for rehearsal at 7 o'clock tomorrow." Ray, still a teenager, showed up to find Dizzy, pianist Bud Powell, Max Roach, and Charlie "Bird" Parker—leading lights of the bebop revolution. A couple of weeks later, the vibes player Milt Jackson joined the group. For the next two years, Milt and Ray shared a room, traveling with Dizzy's band. Singer Ella Fitzgerald joined the band in the 1940s. She and Ray fell in love, and in 1948 they married.

Deep Down in Music

Dizzy would later explain Ray Brown's greatness as a bassist by telling a writer that Brown was always inquisitive about music. Brown wanted to know why one chord and not another was chosen. Dizzy thought he was "the strongest, most fluid and imaginative bassist in modern jazz at that time, with the exception of Oscar Pettiford."[10]

Brown, who had never studied bass, sought out symphonic bass players in every major city he visited and took lessons with them. It was not an ideal way to study—on the run—but it was the only method he could devise, with his schedule. Brown's accomplishment as a performer was all the more remarkable because in those days he played without amplifiers. "You had to put the strings up high [over the bridge], and the gut strings broke a lot when it got hot, if you had acid in your perspiration. But somehow we got it done," he reminisced.[11] (The strings used to be made of catgut; now they're made of metal or plastic.)

Brown led a trio that accompanied Ella Fitzgerald from 1948 until 1951. But he didn't want to play as his wife's accompanist forever; the art of the singer's accompanist on any instrument is limited to support. Brown wanted to explore adventurous, instrumental music. When Oscar Peterson, a great jazz pianist, asked Brown to join an instrumental trio and tour with the Jazz at the Philharmonic organization—a leading showcase for jazz musicians—Brown longed to do so. Ella insisted he stay with her. The conflict over their careers put too much stress on the marriage, and they divorced in 1952.

In Peterson's group, and later as a group leader himself, Brown won many polls and Grammy Awards and countless salutes from other musicians, critics, and fans. Though he worked with many groups, he probably never outdid his artistry and sensitivity as an ensemble player and a soloist on such albums as *The Trio: Live From Chicago*, recorded with Oscar Peterson at the London House in 1961. All the albums Brown did in Peterson's trios are thrilling. The depth and resonance of his sound with the trio provided a standard by which other bassists measure themselves.

In the 1960s, when Brown was touring in Japan, a fledgling bassist, Rufus Reid, who was stationed there in the U.S. Navy, fell in love with his playing and followed him around for weeks. In England, another young

ay Brown

bassist, Dave Holland, who would be hired in the late 1960s by Miles Davis, listened to Brown's recordings endlessly for instruction and inspiration. Many young musicians fell in love with Brown's artistry and became convinced they might have brilliant futures as creative bassists. Brown had proved it could be done.

In 1966, Brown went to Hollywood, where he played all kinds of music in the studios for albums, movies, and television shows. He was asked to play for some of the most important and popular projects, including the Quincy Jones recording "Killer Joe," the film *Bird*, and the Natalie Cole album *Unforgettable*, which lifted her career to its greatest heights.

He and his second wife, Cecilia, settled in California. After nearly twenty years as a studio player, he decided to concentrate on writing and arranging for his own group. He took talented young players under his wing and toured the world with them. He loved to perform before live audiences. It was much more challenging than studio work, he thought.

Bassists always considered Brown a master teacher by his example on recordings beginning in the 1940s. By the 1960s, because of the great development of the bass as a timekeeping, harmonic, and soloing instrument in the hands of Pettiford and Brown, and a few other very strong players, a flowering of bassists began.

7
PROMINENT SIDEMEN AND LEADERS

The bebop pianists concentrated on developing the harmonic and melodic capacities of their instrument. The drummers played more complicated rhythms. It was left to the bassists in the agile, emotionally expressive, musically exploratory groups to free the pianist's left hand from its timekeeping role, to provide a continuous, rhythmic, forward movement, and to play melodies that contrasted and interacted with the basic melody lines of songs.

Best remembered for their work as sidemen are such bassists as Tommy Potter, Curly Russell, John Simmons, Gene Ramey, Sam Jones, Gene Taylor, George Morrow, Wilbur Ware, Percy Heath, Paul Chambers, Butch Morris, Doug Watkins, and Eugene Wright. They gave indispensable support to groups led by Dizzy Gillespie, Charlie Parker, Thelonious Monk, Dave Brubeck, Sonny Rollins,

John Coltrane, and others from the 1940s into the 1960s—the groups in the bebop revolution and after.

George Duvivier: One of the greatest bassists to work as a sideman, Duvivier played in the recording studios for much of his career. He worked in clubs and concerts, too, and prided himself on writing arrangements. Duvivier's strong, intelligent, beautiful playing inspired Edward Berger to write a book about him, called *Bassically Speaking*. It portrays a musician who drove himself to excel—to study, perform, and pioneer at a time when African-Americans were just beginning to find acceptance in the studios. Too often it was assumed that African-Americans couldn't read music well enough to play at the level needed in the studios. Duvivier helped destroy that myth, and he brightened the prospects for other African-American musicians.

Tommy Potter played on the famous Dial and Savoy sessions with Charlie "Bird" Parker's groups in the 1940s. He became involved with the inner circle of beboppers, and after working with Parker on his famous early recordings, he found himself in demand with many well-known musicians.

Curly Russell, who also worked with Bird, began playing professionally with swing bands on the road. In the 1940s, arriving back in his native New York, he found Dizzy and Bird playing at the Three Deuces on 52nd Street. Russell played bass with them. A fine timekeeper with a tone that carried throughout the music, Russell played with other important musicians in the 1940s and 1950s, among them Miles Davis, Coleman Hawkins, Bud Powell, and Thelonious Monk.

John Simmons, who was born in Los Angeles, got his start with swing-era groups in the 1930s. When he made his way to Chicago, Benny Goodman, Louis Armstrong, and many other very prominent musicians of the era recognized his gift and hired him. Simmons worked with Thelonious Monk in the late 1940s and with Tadd Dameron, an important arranger for the beboppers, in the 1950s.

Sam Jones, who was born in Florida, played with the popular alto saxophonist Cannonball Adderley from 1959 through 1965, and then with Oscar Peterson's trio for about six years. He was also in demand for groups and recordings with Duke Ellington, pianist Bill Evans, vibist Milt Jackson, guitarist Wes Montgomery, alto saxophonist Johnny Hodges (a leading light of Duke Ellington's band), alto saxophonist Sonny Stitt (a disciple of Bird), trumpeter and fluegelhornist Art Farmer, and pianist Red Garland.

In 1960, he won the *Down Beat* Critics Poll. From 1961 through 1964, he was the bassist in *Playboy's* All Star Jazz Poll. In 1969, he was selected as musician of the year in Copenhagen, Denmark, a country that especially reveres jazz. In the 1970s, he played with leading jazz pianists Bobby Timmons, Wynton Kelly, Cedar Walton, and Duke Jordan. Jones's sound, beat, and ideas impressed younger players such as Rufus Reid. When Rufus found himself discouraged by the inferior quality of other musicians, or sometimes just by the difficulties inherent in life and the music scene, he would go to hear Sam Jones play in Bradley's, a leading piano-bass duo room in New York. Then he felt refreshed and inspired again about life and music.

Paul Chambers had a similar effect on younger players. In his teens in Pittsburgh, Pennsylvania, where he was born in 1935, he worked with guitarist Kenny Burrell and other local jazz players. At age twenty, Chambers went to New York, where he was accepted by busy players. He performed at an elegant supper club, the Embers, on the Upper East Side, and at Birdland, which was called "the jazz corner of the world."

In 1955, he played with trombonists J. J. Johnson, an exciting musician who emerged during the bebop era, and Kai Winding. Later that year, Chambers joined Miles Davis's quintet, working first with pianist Red Garland and drummer Philly Joe Jones. Spending eight years in the group, Chambers played with many great musicians and recorded several of Davis's most important albums. Other bassists adored him for his strong walking bass style and fine tone.

By 1963, he was playing in Miles's group with pianist Wynton Kelly and drummer Jimmy Cobb. Kelly was suffering from epilepsy, and Chambers, too, was in bad health. But the rhythm section had one of the

George Duvivier

healthiest sounds imaginable. The three men left Miles's group in 1963 but stayed together, touring as a trio and recording for a while with a masterful guitarist, Wes Montgomery. Chambers died in 1969. Two years later, Kelly died. Jimmy Cobb, who had tried to help them through their bouts with illnesses, never forgot the sound of the sensational rhythm section that he had been proud to play in.

Leroy Vinnegar: Of special note for his strong swinging, walking bass style, Vinnegar, born in Indianapolis, Indiana, played in the house band at the popular Bee Hive club on Chicago's South Side in the 1950s. Lured by the beauty of Los Angeles and the activity on the jazz scene, he made it his home base from 1954 into the 1980s. He was hired by the popular tenor saxophonist Stan Getz, trumpeter Shorty Rogers, pianist Herb Geller, trumpeter and singer Chet Baker, and saxophonist Serge Chaloff. Vinnegar also worked with drummer Shelly Manne and world-renowned pianist André Previn in a trio that recorded a best-selling jazz album, *My Fair Lady*, in 1956. It's interesting to note that all these musicians were white (Vinnegar was African-American); the jazz world was the first sector of American society to become integrated.

Other bass players loved the strength of Vinnegar's sound and traditional style. But by the late 1960s, the music scene was changing. Modern bassists, who played melodic solos, and electric bass players began getting the jobs. Vinnegar's forte was the foundation. In the 1980s, he moved to Portland, Oregon, a favorite city with many creative artists. "I felt burned out, like there was no where else I could go in L.A.," he said.[1] He found excellent musicians to play with at regular gigs, and he was happy to begin a new life.

In the 1980s, Vinnegar did the CD *Walkin' the Basses*, the first recording he had led in seventeen years. The album celebrated the style that had made his work tantamount to a fundamental course in bass playing. Christian McBride, the leading bass star in New York in 1995, whose versatility and thorough virtuosity went far beyond Vinnegar's style, had studied Vinnegar's playing on his earlier albums. "I listened to Leroy a lot," McBride told jazz writer Zann Stewart. Stewart included the comment in the liner notes for *Walkin' the Basses*. "He's bad," McBride said, giving the ultimate tribute.[2] ("Bad" among jazz players means good, powerful.)

Also prominent on the West Coast beginning in the 1940s was **George "Red" Callender,** whose autobiography, *Unfinished Dream*, the title of a song he wrote, provides great insight into his success.

Born in Haynesville, Virginia, in March 1916 and raised in Atlantic City, New Jersey, he had to battle a group of white kids who called him racist names. He also suffered from a strict public school teacher who whacked him across the knuckles with a pointer if he didn't sing correctly. But she couldn't kill his sense of joy in music.

At night, the radio brought him the sound of Duke Ellington's band. "I was thrilled with what [trumpeter] Bubber Miley was doing with his plunger mute, though it was the low sounds which appealed to me the most. . . . The Mills Brothers [a very popular singing group] had started their live broadcasts and I felt a real affinity for John Mills, who sang bass."[3]

He had already earned the nickname "Red," for his flaming red hair and freckles contrasting with his brown skin, by the time he went to a military academy, Bordentown, near Trenton, New Jersey. A music teacher there recognized his budding talent and "awakened me to the possibilities in the world of music," Red recalled. Red was soon playing tuba in Bordentown's band. "I was so in love with the music that I developed the habit of getting up at four A.M. every morning to practise for a few hours before beginning the daily routine," he recalled. The teacher challenged him to play difficult music. When Red protested, the teacher encouraged him, saying, "I know you can play it. Just try."[4]

A classmate found a bass in his closet at home and sold it to Red for fifteen dollars. His teacher helped by giving him an instruction booklet. For the rest of his life, Red would play both tuba and bass. "The first thing I learned [on the bass] was the popular hit, 'Careless Love,' which could be played all in the first position, key of F. . . . I joined the dance orchestra with my bass and tuba. . . . All that was necessary to play the

Paul Chambers

popular dance tunes were the first two positions. A few years elapsed before I studied the instrument to learn the first six positions. . . . My fingers were so sore, I kept them wrapped in tape. Bass strings were still being made of gut then. To play loud and strong enough to be heard over the drums required a toughness that I had to develop. Strength in the fingers, especially the fourth finger of the left hand, took years to build."[5]

Painstakingly he learned to improvise. "My ear was good, but improvisation takes knowledge as well as freedom," he said.[6] Eventually he thought he would be able to play jazz. Moving to New York City, he took odd jobs and went to jazz clubs to hear great swing-era bands at Harlem's Savoy Ballroom. He especially liked the bassist in Claude Hopkins's band, because the man played high up on the neck of the instrument. Most players still confined themselves to the first two or three positions low down on the bass. And some were still slapping the bass. "That's something I've always refused to do," Red said.[7]

A friend was offered the bassist's job in a touring band, but his parents wouldn't let him go on the road, so Red was offered the job. When he asked for his mother's permission, she said, "Why yes. God will take care of you."[8] Her great faith gave Red a special boost. Red began making connections and developing friendships with other young jazz musicians. In one city, he found a piano in his rooming house and decided to start composing. "My first effort was called 'Unfinished Dream.' . . . One of the main reasons I wanted to become a proficient writer was to disprove the then popular myth that bass players and drummers didn't know anything about music."[9]

Eventually, as bassist for a show called *Brownskin Models*, he landed in Los Angeles. He fell in love with the city and decided to stay. He was concentrating on playing in tune and on using his muscles to produce a big sound. "This was before the days of amplification and there were no wires," he noted.[10]

In 1937, he was asked on short notice to play with Louis Armstrong's band at the Vogue Ballroom to replace Pops Foster, who was sick. Red then recorded "The Sunny Side of the Street" and "Once in a While" at the Decca studios. "Suddenly I was on two hit tunes. . . . [T]he name of Red Callender became known to thousands," he reminisced. "Shortly after the Vogue Ballroom gig, my phone started ringing and has never really stopped."[11]

In his early years in Los Angeles, he met his idol, Jimmy Blanton, and a budding saxophonist, Buddy Collette. Red and Buddy befriended a younger musician, Charles Mingus. Mingus asked Callender for lessons. Red became a mentor, a teacher, and even a father figure for Mingus, who came from a troubled background. At that time, Red didn't know that Mingus would become one of the most important jazz bassists and composers.

Red was invited to join Duke's band after Jimmy Blanton died, but he decided not to accept. "I didn't want to play 'Jack the Bear' and all those things Blanton had made famous. I wasn't even sure I could fill Blanton's shoes. There was my tuba playing, my composing, arranging and recording activities to pursue. Knowing that Duke actually wanted me was quite enough for my ego."[12]

Red also worked to integrate the segregated musicians' union locals. Playing regularly for television studio orchestras, he became the second African-American hired for a television studio band on the West Coast. NBC hired him to go on staff in California in 1964. He was the first African-American to have that job. He worked for CBS, too, and was featured in bands for many hit shows. A renowned teacher by the 1980s, he founded the Wind College in Los Angeles and continued his whirl of performing jobs into the 1990s. In demand until the end, he died in his seventies.

Percy Heath, who became the bassist in the Modern Jazz Quartet in the 1950s, grew up in a musical family in Philadelphia, Pennsylvania. His younger brothers were Jimmy, a saxophonist, and Albert, nicknamed Tootie, a drummer. In 1946, Percy moved to New York, played bass in bebop groups, and in 1951 joined vibes player Milt Jackson's quartet. It turned out to be the most important event in Percy's professional life.

Deep Down in Music

The next year the group was renamed the Modern Jazz Quartet. Its permanent members by 1955 were John Lewis, a pianist steeped in classical music; Connie Kay, a subtle drummer whose sensitivity proved excellent for a chamber music group; Heath; and Jackson. Heath fit in well because of his command of the bass's responsibility for combining harmony and a continuous rhythmic pulse. Jackson was the spontaneous, loose, adventuresome player. Without his swing, the group would never have achieved the effervescence that stayed in touch with the blues roots of jazz.

In the 1950s, the MJQ, as it was called, had a fresh, otherworldly sound unique in jazz. And it came along when the bebop revolution had run its course. Musicians and audiences were looking for a new sound. The MJQ was always called a Third Stream or cool jazz group, combining European and jazz traditions so effectively that it had broad appeal, delighting both jazz and European classical music fans.

And the MJQ insisted on wearing formal clothes for performances, putting the finishing touch of classiness on its exciting, airy style. When the men signed a contract with Atlantic Records in the 1950s, the group was off and running to become one of the world's most popular jazz groups. It suffered a long but temporary dip in fortunes during the reign of rock in the 1970s. But in the early 1980s, the American music scene changed again, as it does about every ten years. Acoustic jazz was becoming trendy and appealing once more. And the MJQ was lionized as an immortal group, playing in concert halls, high-priced jazz clubs, and New York's Café Carlyle, an upper-class, society-oriented supper club.

Eugene Wright was the bassist in pianist Dave Brubeck's quartet, a group that in the 1950s appealed to a collegiate crowd. It, too, played a cool jazz style, an offshoot of bebop. But Brubeck was a percussive player whose counterrhythms gave his music a sense of complexity and excitement, while his alto saxophonist, Paul Desmond, played a light, lyrical, swinging lead.

Brubeck's group became financially successful before the MJQ did. In

Percy Heath, bassist for the
Modern Jazz Quartet

November 1954, Brubeck was portrayed on the cover of *Time* magazine. Drummer Joe Morello along with Brubeck provided a gritty foil for the melodic beauty of Desmond's horn lines. And Eugene Wright had a gift for dependable timekeeping and choosing the best notes to embellish the chords. With Morello, Wright provided the launching pad for Brubeck and Desmond. Their wildly popular recordings such as "Take Five" made the group one of the most successful jazz groups in history.

Niels-Henning Orsted Pedersen: George Duvivier, who never ceased trying to educate himself, to improve and modernize his work, had a great shock in the 1960s when he heard European bassist Niels-Henning Orsted Pedersen in person. Orsted Pedersen, who had fallen in love with jazz and dropped his classical music studies, was plucking the bass strings with two and three fingers, not just one finger, as traditional bassists did. Duvivier was not to be outdone — he immediately taught himself to play with two and three fingers as well. Most modern bass players did the same thing.

As bassist and teacher Cecil McBee explains it, bass players began playing pizzicato by using just the index finger to pluck the strings. A lot of flesh of the index finger was employed to produce the largest sound possible from the string. When players started to use two fingers, to accent tonalities and add grace notes, both the index and second fingers were at a greater angle to the strings. There's less flesh in contact with the strings. A player can produce faster, sharper notes using two or more fingers. But the big, fat sound of a plucked bass string comes from a player using only one finger.

When a player uses three fingers, all of them are placed absolutely perpendicular to the strings. Only the fleshy tips of the fingers are used to pluck the strings. A player gets the greatest speed that way. Orsted Pedersen and Duvivier were advancing the melodic potential of the instrument.

Israel Crosby: Steeped in the tradition of the swing era, Crosby began playing melodic, hornlike lines in the 1930s and 1940s with many well-known jazz musicians. But it's for his work with pianist Ahmad Jamal, especially from 1957 to 1962, that Crosby is best remembered. Jamal's trio had hit recordings with such songs as "Poinciana," on the album *At the Pershing: But Not for Me*. Jamal was renowned for giving his sidemen space to solo. The pauses in the romantic, swinging music created a sense of suspense and drama. Crosby's style was exciting, inventive, and melodic.

From Jamal's trio, Crosby went to play in another very popular group led by pianist George Shearing in 1962. Unfortunately, Crosby became sick that year. He went home to Chicago, where he died of a heart attack at the age of forty-three.

Willie Ruff is an African-American bassist who took his talent from his birthplace in the Deep South to Yale University. He became an accomplished classical and jazz player on both string bass and French horn. He and pianist Dwike Mitchell have performed as a duo for many years. At Yale, with his excellent connections, Ruff became influential despite his separation from the mainstream playing arena for jazz.

Keith Moore "Red" Mitchell, who was born on September 20, 1927, grew up in Radburn, New Jersey, an all-white suburb of New York. He wanted to become an inventor, but he fell in love with jazz when he heard a Count Basie record in 1943. So Red (nicknamed for his flaming red hair) started taking the bus to 52nd Street and to Harlem. "The jazz world was a much nicer world than I was used to," he recalled about those days. "People introduced me to musicians. We talked about music. The scene was integrated in every way. I loved it."[13]

He became a bebop devotee. When he went to Cornell University to study electrical engineering, he kept heading to the piano in the library to practice bebop. Drafted into the army and sent to Germany in 1946, he bought a bass in exchange for twelve cartons of cigarettes at seventy cents a carton, and he practiced the bass around the clock. Though he admired Slam Stewart and Oscar Pettiford, he had learned from listening to Ray Brown that a bassist could play sophisticated bebop lines, too.

Back in New York after his discharge from the army, Red tried to please his parents by using the GI Bill to study bass and music appreciation at Juilliard. The school did not yet have a jazz program, however, so he left school, moved to a midtown hotel with other young jazz "cats," and sat in on 52nd Street. Often, all he could afford to eat was a hot dog/potato knish/coffee lunch for twenty-five cents. In a 52nd Street club he found a job for fifteen dollars a week. There he met Charlie Parker and Miles Davis. Bird terrified Red by asking him to sit in with his group. Afterward, Miles Davis complimented Red and invited him to rehearse with a band that would later record Miles's album *Birth of the Cool*.

By December 1949, Red had joined Woody Herman's band and led the one-night-stand life until January 1951. "I got the same strain of tuberculosis that killed . . . Jimmy Blanton," Red recalled. "But streptomycin had been developed. So I survived. One nighters, with no sleep, with stress and poor food, killed the majority of my contemporaries."

When he recovered, he answered a call to work in a Los Angeles club for two months in a group led by Red Norvo, a vibes player. Red Mitchell wasn't supposed to travel constantly anymore, but he could work steadily in one city. Finding his way into the Los Angeles studios, he became a popular bass player at MGM Studios because of his flexibility. "You had to play anything they put in front of you, even rock on electric bass, which I did for almost ten years. We never knew whether it was going to be 'The Marriage of Figaro Overture' or whatever. The height of my rock career was a Coca-Cola commercial with Ray Charles, which became a hit." As one of the first African-American musicians in the California studios, Red helped break down the color line there. Ray Brown began playing in the studios because of Red's support.

He worked with many composers, beginning with Henry Mancini, who wrote music that required Red to cover the big distances on the fingerboard quickly. Red decided to tune his bass in fifths, A-G-D-C, the way a cellist tunes his instrument, instead of fourths, G-D-A-E, the traditional way bassists tune. Very few bassists have ever followed Red's lead. But he thought his system expanded the range of the instrument so he could play more notes. He also thought he improved the tone of the bass and made its sound bigger. "Plus you can play chords," he added. Composer and orchestra leader André Previn was shocked but pleased when Red played with his new tuning system in the studios.

Red's playing was so strong that when he played in duos with pianists, he could often be heard leading the music rather than playing accompaniment. Sometimes the result was an intriguing chamber jazz performance. The instruments sang to each other, questioning and answering. The brilliant contemporary pianist Kenny Barron fared well as a partner with Red. Sometimes, though, Red overwhelmed other jazz pianists with whom he was paired. He dominated the improvisation. It's probable that, with a touch of the rebel in his character and with his complete confidence, sometimes overconfidence, in his own ideas, Red devised his own tuning system to satisfy his old urge to become an inventor.

Touring in Stockholm, Sweden, in 1954, Red fell in love with its cleanliness and the "honesty and fairness" of the people, he said. He asked a cabdriver where the slums were. The driver said there weren't any. Red spent the next fourteen years reading about Sweden. In 1968, he decided to move to Stockholm, promising himself to play only jazz and improvise lyrics while he played. He was always in demand to play. Every year, he returned to perform in the United States for a few months. He died suddenly while on tour in Oregon in 1992.

POPS FOSTER

THE JAZZ BASS TREE

This outline focuses on the pivotal bassists throughout the twentieth century. Some were the best players and/or greatest innovators in their eras, and all succeeding generations have inherited their riches.

THE SLAP BASSISTS FROM NEW ORLEANS, 1900-1939

Pops Foster is the best-known early slap bassist because he did so much recording. He slapped his bass and played a thump-thump rhythm for the walking bass line, combining the rhythm and the root note of chords.

Other early slap bassists, some of whom painted their basses in bright colors and spun them for entertainment, were **Bill Johnson, Steve Brown, John Lindsay, Wellman Braud, Billy Taylor Sr.,** and **Chink Martin.** Bill Johnson, the eldest of this group, may have been the first slap bassist. All of them left their native South, headed west and north, and joined the big bands in the swing era during the 1920s and 1930s.

1934–1947

The big-band bassists learned from listening to Blanton's records with Ellington. Among Blanton's most important contemporaries in the big-band era, which lasted until about 1947, was *Milt Hinton* in Cab Calloway's band. Hinton began by playing slap bass, but with his education in classical violin techniques and his understanding of harmonies, he adapted Blanton's innovations and influenced many younger players.

MILT HINTON

1939–1941

Jimmy Blanton, who joined Duke Ellington's band in 1939, played long, fluid lines as the horn players did, for a walking bass line. With a fine under-

JIMMY BLANTON

standing of harmonies, he explored the possibilities for bassists as featured soloists. Blanton died in 1942. By that time, he had influenced every bassist of his own era and yet to come.

1930s TO 1950s

Slam Stewart, who began as a classical violinist and switched to the double bass in the late 1930s, was influenced by Jimmy Blanton and Milt Hinton, too. Stewart became a star in the team of Slim and Slam, with pianist Slim Gaillard, as the era of the small combo began in the early 1940s. Later, he became an important member of an illustrious trio led by virtuosic pianist Art Tatum, with Tiny Grimes on guitar.

1940s AND 1950s

Oscar Pettiford, who was mightily impressed by Blanton, carried the torch further along after Blanton's death. He became a star in early bebop groups, and with his big sound and forceful swing, exerted a great influence over his contemporaries in the 1940s and 1950s.

1940s TO PRESENT

Ray Brown Jr. listened to Blanton, Hinton, and Pettiford for instruction and in turn became one of the most important influences in contemporary bass playing. His first important job was

OSCAR PETTIFORD

RAY BROWN

with Dizzy Gillespie's group in the late 1940s, in which his gifts for swing and harmonic embellishment established him as a standard-bearer. To develop as a musician, he studied with classical players whenever he could as he traveled around the world in the 1940s and 1950s. By

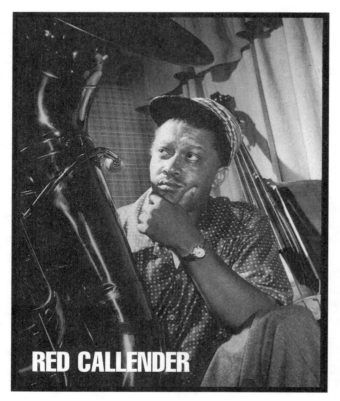

RED CALLENDER

the 1960s, he settled in California and was a popular bassist in the studios, until he returned to touring with his own group in the 1980s and 1990s.

Red Callender in Los Angeles was one of the first African-Americans to play in the Los Angeles studios.

Red Mitchell, a white bassist who grew up under the spell of the big bands and the bebop groups, and a technically advanced and innovative player for the way he tuned his bass, helped Ray Brown Jr., an African-American, find work in the Los Angeles studios.

Leroy Vinnegar, with a strong, classic walking bass and supportive technique, became a very popular player in the studios there, too, but later he began to lose work to the demand for double bass soloists and electric bassists.

FROM THE 1950s

George Duvivier and *Milt Hinton* became very popular double bass players in the New York studios during the 1950s and 1960s. Duvivier was in demand until his death in the 1980s. Hinton has continued working as a major attraction into his eighties in the 1990s.

FROM THE 1960s

Ron Carter, famous for his adventures in harmonies and swing during the 1960s as a member of trumpeter Miles Davis's groups, set new standards for double bass players. Carter, who has degrees from conservatories and universities, writes books, teaches, and exerts his influence over musicians on all instruments.

Richard Davis, a professor of music at the University of Wisconsin at Madison, became a role model for his ability to play with virtuosity in classical and jazz groups.

Scott LaFaro, who became the bassist in pianist Bill Evans's group

RON CARTER

EDDIE GOMEZ

in 1959, set standards for harmonic innovations.

Eddie Gomez, who played with Evans, too, and *Paul Chambers* and *Sam Jones,* who played with important small combos beginning in the 1950s, became role models for their technical virtuosity and harmonic ideas.

In Europe, *Niels-Henning Orsted Pedersen,* who had begun his career as a classical musician, became revered for his fast, swinging, strong technique. Plucking or pulling the strings with three fingers, he sent such great players as George Duvivier to the woodshed to play with the same technique—a boon for speed.

Charles Mingus, who was a protégé of Red Callender, distinguished himself as a strong, wildly adventurous player, improviser, and composer—one of the most important composers in jazz. Categorized as a free jazz player—one no longer confined to improvising on the chords of written songs in the bebop style, or on modes or a series of notes within a scale as Miles Davis and then saxophonist John Coltrane

CHARLES MINGUS

did—Mingus became an inspiration to young players who became totally involved with free jazz.

Among his protégés has been *Charlie Haden,* whose reputation as an eclectic player and composer became particularly bright in the 1990s.

CHARLIE HADEN

RUFUS REID

FROM THE 1970s

By the 1960s, an important new generation of bassists was developing. Among the best players, who were influenced by all the above-named players, as well as some of their contemporaries, are *Rufus Reid, Cecil McBee, Ray Drummond, George Mraz, Michael Moore,* and *Dave Holland.* They remained faithful to the jazz traditions while establishing their own adventurous ideas and groups playing modern music.

Electric bass players became very important with the rise of rock and roll in the 1960s and 1970s. *Monk Montgomery* is believed to have been the first acoustic jazz bassist to begin playing electric bass, when he received a present of a Fender bass.

Jaco Pastorius is usually described as the greatest of all the electric bass players in jazz. He was primarily known for his work in rock and roll. The worlds of the electric and acoustic players have remained separate, with their own stars. Some players, however, have crossed back and forth—among the well known have been *Steve Swallow, Bob Cranshaw,* and *Bob Hurst.*

CHRISTIAN McBRIDE

FROM THE 1980s

Inheriting the wealth of experience and artistry of all the historic players, young acoustic bassists in the 1980s and 1990s struggled to build reputations as leaders and great support players simultaneously.

Among the best known are *Avery Sharpe,* an illustrious bassist in pianist McCoy Tyner's group; *Santi Debriano,* who has close ties to both Latin and traditional American jazz; *Peter Washington,* who began playing in the limelight with Art Blakey and the Jazz Messengers in the 1980s and eventually replaced George Mraz in pianist Tommy Flanagan's stellar trio; and *Christian McBride*, who plays both as a sideman and a leader.

In the 1960s and then again in the 1980s and 1990s, there was an obvious flowering of fine acoustic bassists, as techniques for amplifying the bass have permitted the musicians to make its voice heard with great clarity and strength.

8

CHARLES MINGUS— GENIUS AND MADMAN

harles Mingus, who was born in Nogales, Arizona, on April 22, 1922, soon moved to Los Angeles, where his family life was confusing and unsettling. His father, a post office worker, was a domineering man who often beat the children fiercely. At the same time, he was also very protective of his children against outsiders. He didn't let anyone, not even the teachers in school, do anything to harm or insult them. "Daddy was next to God and even sometimes told God what to do: 'God damn it!' he'd say when he got good and angry," Charles recalled in his fascinating autobiography, *Beneath the Underdog*.[1]

Charles began playing cello in elementary school bands, where he was considered very gifted. But he didn't have an adequate teacher. In high school, he could not read complicated music in band rehearsals. The leader

90

blamed Charles's shortcomings on his race. That type of prejudice dogged African-Americans for many years. Another kid in the band, Buddy Collette, then playing clarinet, encouraged Charles to start playing the bass.

Charles was chubby, pigeon-toed, and bowlegged. Bullies picked on him. He learned to defend himself so well that he became the aggressor at times. Once he took off his belt and began waving it around his head, scaring away a pack of African-American boys who were threatening him. Charles got into scrapes and fights with white kids, too. He felt that danger always lurked around the corner. These incidents and memories would upset him for the rest of his life.

He took Buddy Collette's advice to switch to bass. Charles's father traded in the cello and paid an additional $130 for a brand-new German-made double bass. Through another young musician whom Charles knew, trombonist Britt Woodman, Charles got the phone number of bassist Joe Comfort. All these boys grew up to become distinguished jazz players. Comfort taught Charles how to tune his bass and to practice by accompanying the bands he heard on the radio. But Comfort, who could play any instrument by ear, did not teach Charles to read music.

Then Woodman told Charles about a new bassist in town, Red Callender. "Man, I had a rehearsal for a record with the greatest bass player possible! He sounded like a horn," Woodman told Charles before taking him to a rehearsal of the Les Hite band.[2] Callender was playing there. Charles persisted in asking Red for lessons, and finally Red, still a student himself, agreed to teach him. "That was typical of him; Mingus would go through walls to get what he wanted," Red said. "What I taught him primarily was how to get a sound from the instrument. However, even then, he knew exactly what he aspired to be—the world's greatest bass player. That was his all-consuming passion.

"To prove that genius is hard work, Mingus practised seventeen, eighteen hours a day. I'd drive by his house early in the morning and there would be Mingus, out on his front porch, practising. That's the secret of his greatness; the hours he put into it. . . . After a few years with me, I suggested that he study with [my teachers]. By then he was

Charles Mingus

also into composing."[3] Red's teachers, who also helped Mingus with his technique, were a man named H. Rheinschagen, a former bass player in the New York Philharmonic Orchestra, and Lloyd Reese, who directed his own conservatory in Los Angeles and trained several famous musicians.

Many years later, Mingus became famous in the jazz world for the passion and strength of his playing, the compositions he wrote, and the performances he wrested from the musicians in his groups, Callender would recall. "His object in music was to astound everyone, his idea about writing was to intimidate the players with [music] so hard that it was almost impossible to play."[4]

Callender knew that Mingus lost his temper with people who didn't play his music the way he wanted. Sometimes Mingus actually hit the men in his group; he socked a fine trombonist onstage. Mingus was so uninhibited that he ordered audiences to be quiet, and if people made too much noise, he would eat a meal onstage or stop playing altogether.

He attracted a great deal of criticism for his daring music, which sounded strange and chaotic in the days before people became more appreciative of the growing freedom in jazz compositions. The music was often very beautiful and moving. Mingus never remained in the background of any group. Raucous and rough as a performer, he always asserted himself as an equal with the front-line musicians. His finesse was in his emotionality.

To try to escape from record companies that paid musicians poorly, Mingus formed his own label, Debut, and made several records on it. The most important one was done at a concert at Massey Hall in Toronto, Canada, in May 1953.

The concert, billed as The Greatest Jazz Concert Ever, also starred Dizzy Gillespie, Charlie "Bird" Parker, pianist Bud Powell, and drummer Max Roach—the vanguard of the bebop revolution. Unfortunately, though, the paychecks to the musicians bounced, and Mingus gave the Debut label to his second wife as a divorce settlement. But the recording signaled to the jazz world that Mingus had arrived as a forceful modern bassist. In 1953, he went to work for Duke Ellington's band briefly as a replacement for Oscar Pettiford. Mingus got into a fight with Duke's gifted, eccentric trombonist, Juan Tizol, and had to leave the band. The next year, Mingus formed the Jazz Composers' Workshop and began to develop innovative ideas for the bass's role in jazz while adapting Duke Ellington's compositional standards.

With his own small groups, Mingus began to assert his greatness. Between 1956 and 1961, recording for Atlantic, he showed off his brave new concepts and adventuresome music on "Haitian Fight Song," an aggressive song; "Pithecanthropus Erectus," meant to tell the story of the rise and fall of the human race; "Passions of a Man," another potent, extended composition; and "Good Bye Pork Pie Hat," a tribute to the great tenor saxophonist Lester Young, who had died of alcoholism in 1958. Mingus's power sprang from the boiling cauldron of emotions that he poured into his vibrant playing.

By the 1960s, he was performing and recording with Eric Dolphy, a very gifted alto saxophone and flute player. Together, the two great players created music of ecstatic intensity and lyricism. Their recordings are among some of Mingus's finest.

In 1962, Mingus, Duke Ellington, and Max Roach got together for a trio album, *Money Jungle*. It gave Duke a chance to play piano away from his band, and the album presented Mingus in all his strength and flexibility. He left behind the ideas of strict tempo and meter and achieved new textures, effects, and melodies.

Duke Ellington described the recording session for *Money Jungle*. He had been asked to play his own music in the trio with Mingus and Roach, who were leaders of their own groups. Duke decided to make the recording without rehearsals and with everyone "intent upon togetherness." He told Mingus and Roach that the song "La Fleurette Africaine" should exemplify an African idea: A little flower grows in a part of the jungle where no one ever ventures; though no one sees it, the flower keeps growing more beautiful every day.

"They both gave a nod of understanding. I went to the piano and called to the engineer, 'Roll it!' Roach's rhythmic embellishments could not have been more fitting, nor have sounded more authentic, while Mingus, with his eyes closed, fell into each and every harmonic groove, adding counter-melodies as though he had been playing the number all his life. It was one of those mystic moments when our three muses were one and the same. There was just one take, and I was thrilled."[5]

Young musicians who would become stars long after Mingus died recalled the impact of his style. Upon first hearing his records, many thought it was too rough and even erratic rhythmically. They wanted to be smoother players. But Ray Drummond, for example, thought Mingus could execute nearly everything he could imagine trying to play. Christian McBride, who was born long after Mingus played at Massey Hall, was thrilled by the recording of that concert. Mingus sounded so powerful that McBride thought, "Oh, man, I wonder if everyone plays like this."[6] Another bassist, Kenny Davis, realized the bass could function out front, not just as a background instrument, when he heard that album. Ron Carter liked Mingus's compositional skills and his influence on other musicians' performances. Mingus varied tempos, sometimes within the same song, for expressiveness. He wrote extended pieces, leaving behind the traditional forms of the blues and American popular songs. And he required collective improvising—everyone improvising at the same time—that resulted in atonal music from his group. He played unusual notes as an harmonic device to produce a special tone and feeling.

Mingus recorded a great deal in the early to mid-1960s. After that, he became aware that he was ill with amyotrophic lateral sclerosis, a progressively disabling neurological disease (known as Lou Gehrig's disease, for the baseball star who died of it in 1941). But he continued to record and to work on his autobiography. He wrote hundreds of pages and struggled for several years to find a publisher.

He recorded the album *Let My Children Hear Music* in 1971, a big-band session filled with the new freedom he had tried to establish in jazz. He thought the album was one of his best and wrote in the liner notes, "I think the music on this record is serious in every sense. I say, let my children have music. For God's sake, rid this society of some of the noise so that those who have ears will be able to use them someplace listening to good music. When I say good I don't mean that today's music is bad because it is loud. I mean the structures have paid no attention to the past history of the music. Nothing is simple. It's as if people came to Manhattan and acted like it was still full of trees and grass and Indians instead of concrete and tall buildings."[7]

Deep Down in Music

The music shocked some people with its iconoclasm. Mingus had pulled apart some of the existing notions about harmony; it would be at least another decade before general audiences began to accept atonality as beautiful. The songs had fanciful, philosophical titles, such as "The Shoes of the Fisherman's Wife Are Some Jive Ass Slippers" and "Don't Be Afraid, the Clown's Afraid Too." He explained in the liner notes that he preferred to show each musician his part by playing it on the piano or the bass or by singing it instead of writing it down. He wanted the musicians to take those parts and create their own improvisations.

For some tracks on the album, Mingus used large ensembles, including piccolos and bass clarinets in the reed section, French horns, a tuba, six bassists, and a cello. He explained that he was very proud of a lovely song called "Adagio Ma Non Troppo" (Italian for "slowly, but not too slowly") because it expressed his feelings and showed changes in tempo and mood, while the variations on the theme still fit into the one composition. He felt that it had turned out to be as structured as if he had written it on paper. Most of all, the piece showed Mingus's great gift for beautiful melodies. He wrote them as easily as other people drink water.

He died on January 5, 1979, in Cuernavaca, Mexico. His widow, Sue, who was his third wife, has devoted the years since his death to the preservation and performances of his musical legacy, which has grown more influential, respected, and even popular. No one played more powerfully or communicated emotionally stirring ideas better than Mingus. Young players continue to become more virtuosic, and Mingus's music is easier for them to play.

Long after he died, bassists performed his pieces in concerts. New York's Kool Jazz Festival[8] featured a very successful concert starring three virtuosic bassists—Miroslav Vitous, George Mraz, and Ron Carter—in the early 1980s. A group called the Mingus Dynasty recorded Mingus music and performed in clubs. In the 1980s, a jazz orchestra playing his composition "Epitaph" made its debut at Lincoln Center, then toured Europe and the United States and recorded the music, all to great acclaim. A different group, the Mingus Big Band, started playing every Thursday night at Fez, a club in the basement of Manhattan's Time Café, in the early 1990s.

Rufus Reid, who didn't always feel comfortable with the roughness of Mingus's style, nevertheless applauded his innovative ideas. Reid reminded people, "It takes a lot of [courage] for someone to go left when everybody else is going right, and Mingus had that ability."[9] Other bassists found Mingus's humor and bluesy feeling very important.

9

A FLOWERING OF VIRTUOSOS

While Mingus was asserting his might as a leader and composer, many young bassists were working in other people's groups as sidemen. All of them admired Mingus. But to enhance their abilities to solo on the bass, they paid particular attention to horn players, not bassists.

It was extremely important for young bassists to find jobs with illustrious leaders. Carmen McRae, Ella Fitzgerald, Sarah Vaughan, and Betty Carter hired promising youngsters, choosing the ones who could play the bottoms of the chords well. Fledgling bassists often put the finishing touches on their techniques and gained confidence as accompanists for singers. Emerging players hired their contemporaries for groups.

The well-known leaders of instrumental groups were also especially important for young bassists. These leaders gave young players the chance to fill the shoes of the previous generation of bassists who had retired from the playing scene or had become too high-priced for work as sidemen. Pianist George Shearing started his group in the 1950s with the excellent bassist *John Levy*. Levy had played in notable performances such as a concert at Carnegie Hall with the legendary singer Billie Holiday, but he quit playing and became an artists' manager. One of Shearing's young bassists in the late 1970s and early 1980s was *Brian Torff*, who studied at the Berklee College of Music in Boston and the Manhattan School of Music. He played "Tenderly" much the way he had heard Billie Holiday sing it.

Ron Carter

Perhaps the most respected modern bassist is Ron Carter. Born in May 1937 in Ferndale, Michigan, he started on cello and then switched to bass. He acquired classical training at the Eastman School of Music in Rochester, New York. After graduation, he studied at the Manhattan School of Music and played in a variety of groups with stars and young hopefuls. One group was led by the exciting guitarist Wes Montgomery, who played long, complex, harmonically adventurous lines.

In 1963, Ron was hired by trumpeter Miles Davis, the king of cool jazz. In Miles's group, Carter recorded nine wonderful albums. In 1964 alone, he played on *Four and More* and *My Funny Valentine*, recorded at the same concert but released as two different albums, and *Miles Smiles*, acknowledged as among Miles's greatest albums. At that time, Miles's group was playing only acoustic music, and Carter's bass matched the haunting quality of Miles's sound perfectly. His strength, agility, and creativity shine through especially well on the song "Footprints."

Carter played things that the bass players before him had never tried. He was more open harmonically than his predecessors and was pivotal in advancing the sound past its classical roots. Modernism begins with him.

In Miles's group, Carter worked with pianist Herbie Hancock and drummer Tony Williams, both rising stars, to form an innovative rhythm section. Then Ron went on to play for Hancock's albums *Maiden Voyage* in 1965 and *Speak Like a Child* in 1968. Ron also played and recorded with other brilliant modernists in groups called the New York Jazz Quartet and VSOP.

Carter began leading his own groups in 1972. With Kenny Barron as pianist and Ben Riley as drummer, Carter led a group that the sidemen hoped would stay together forever. But Carter disbanded it. The sidemen were inspired to continue to play together, recruiting Buster Williams for a new group called Sphere. Their experience with Carter helped them formulate their artistic goals.

At times, Carter used two bassists in his groups, he playing the piccolo bass and the other bassist using the traditional double bass. The double bassist played the time and the harmony, while Ron took advantage of the freedom to solo on the second bass. But for all his soloing ability, it was, above all, his rhythmic swing that lifted groups out of the ordinary. His concert at Cooper Union's Great Hall in New York in 1982, with pianist Kirk Lightsey and twenty-year-old drummer Marvin "Smitty" Smith, both of whom had an abundance of energy, and a second bassist, swung so much that people nearly danced in the aisles.

Tall, slender, intensely serious, attentive to details, and extremely proud, Carter often played with musicians with far less experience. His reputation gave them the chance to attract audiences. They experienced the thrill and challenge of working with a master. In 1995, his participation in the rhythm section for a CD led by pianist Geri Allen gave her music exceptional vitality. The music swung and moved forward with greater force than the highly subjective Allen, a fascinating young pianist and composer, had ever consistently achieved before.

An even younger pianist, Roberta Piket, who began to emerge in 1995, was delighted when she was asked to play the antique American standard tune "Sweet Lorraine" on the CD *For the Love of Music*, led by swing-era vibist Lionel Hampton. Ron Carter played bass. The arrangement wasn't modern enough for Roberta's taste, but Ron elevated the music for her, "because, instead of just walking a 4/4 bass line, he did things rhythmically that were different from the way anyone else does them," Roberta said. "It's one of his trademarks to play the time differently. And he has a big sound, a big groove, and he makes it easy to swing."[1] Roberta loved the performance.

By 1995, Carter had recorded at least two thousand albums, apart from his career as a performer in concerts, clubs, movies, and videos. He has also taught and written books about playing techniques. Through his life's experience, and with his particular, analytical intelligence, he has a profound understanding of the music business as well as of music. In short, he has earned a reputation as an aristocrat of the bass.

Dave Holland: After Carter, Miles Davis hired Dave Holland, a young Englishman whom Miles heard in a London jazz club. Holland had begun playing electric bass, switched to acoustic, and eventually played both basses for Miles's groups. In 1969, Holland played acoustic while Harvey Brooks played electric bass for Miles's album *Bitches Brew*—a milestone album for bringing on fusion jazz. Pure, acoustic jazz was out of fashion in the late 1960s. Fans worried that jazz was dying or dead. But Miles Davis began using electric instruments and developing the fusion style, and audiences loved it. He had reinvented his career and rescued jazz from oblivion.

In Miles's groups, Holland played electric bass on the albums *Live at the Fillmore* and *Black Beauty*, among others. Holland's hero for bass playing had been Ray Brown. After leaving Miles's band, Holland enjoyed a successful career as a composer and a player in many adventurous groups. One, called Circle, included the famed jazz pianist Chick Corea. Holland also played with Stan Getz for a year and even with Thelonious Monk. He had such great ability that he could fit in with those diverse leaders. From there he went to the Sam Rivers trio, then the Anthony Braxton quartet—very modern groups led by saxophonists. He worked briefly with Betty Carter, the most modern and harmonically adventurous of the old guard jazz singers.

Holland began recording as a leader and soloist on bass and cello in the early 1980s. On his 1988 album, *Triplicate*, with alto saxophonist Steve Coleman and drummer Jack DeJohnette, his strength and propulsive power at least equaled DeJohnette's. He also mastered the cello and recorded a masterpiece of solo playing on his 1982 album, *Life Cycle*.

Steve Swallow, a bright young bassist, began playing in a group led by pianist and arranger George Russell, who was experimenting with ancient music forms for improvisation. At age twenty, Swallow studied with pianist Paul Bley and went on to work with several well-known post-bebop modernists. By the late 1980s, Steve made the bold move of switching from the acoustic bass to the electric bass guitar. He has played with many famous jazz leaders. Highly regarded by his peers, Swallow has recorded impressive duo and trio albums with his wife, pianist Carla Bley, the ex-wife of his former mentor.

Reggie Workman and *Jimmy Garrison* played bass with saxophonist John Coltrane's groups, achieving immortality for their performances on many famous albums.

Richard Davis became prominent as a multifaceted musician who felt equally at home in studios and in classical and jazz groups. Every year from 1966 to 1974 he ranked first in the *Down Beat* magazine critics and readers polls. In those days, he was working as a sideman in many different settings. In 1977, he became a professor of classical music and jazz at the University of Wisconsin at Madison.

Davis played in singer Sarah Vaughan's touring group with pianist Jimmy Jones and drummer Roy Haynes. They made up one of the great rhythm sections in vocal jazz history. He also worked in symphony orchestras under such famous conductors as Leopold Stokowski, Leonard Bernstein, and Igor Stravinsky. In the 1970s, sought after as a studio musician, he played in the Jones-Lewis Orchestra, with which he made recordings. That band played new compositions and arrangements by fluegelhornist and trumpeter Thad Jones every Monday night at the Village Vanguard in New York. Other jazz musicians made it a point to hear that band.

After Davis chose the academic life, he still returned to New York clubs and toured in other cities and countries as leader of his own groups. In 1995, he put together a collection of some of his favorite solos, some released previously, for release on a CD on his own label. One song was called "Reminiscing," written by George Duvivier, on which Davis played the very beautiful melody straightforwardly, with Ben Sidran on piano. Davis had already recorded the song once for an album called *Akari*, released in Japan on the Apollon label, which failed to list Duvivier as the composer.

Davis had other favorites among his own albums and solos, although he didn't own the rights to put them out on his own CD. They included "Bygones and Boogie" on the album *Profiles*, with Gary McFarland; "Santa Barbara and Crenshaw Follies," with a Davis solo, on David Murray's 1986 trio album, *The Hill*; his interpretation of "Summertime" from his own album, *Heavy Sounds*, co-led with drummer Elvin Jones; and "Games," a piece on pianist John Lewis's album *P.O.V.* (which stands for "Point of View"). Also very important to him was "Forest Flower," a song by saxophonist Charles Lloyd, on Richard's own 1977 album, *Harvest*. The music was arranged by bassist Bill Lee, father of the prominent filmmaker Spike Lee.

One more song that was important to Davis was "Animated Suspension," written by bassist Virgil Jones, who had played in Count Basie's band. Richard's version, done in the early 1970s, was recorded with pianist Harold Mabern and drummer Idris Muhammad. His favorite recording dates have a lot to do with the "atmosphere on a recording session," Davis says, "and hearing a story line and creating it."[2]

Scott LaFaro was nineteen when he began playing with pianist Bill Evans in 1959. They met when Evans was paired with LaFaro and drummer Paul Motian to work as the warm-up group for clarinetist Benny Goodman (known as the King of Swing) in a New York club.

Evans, in love with the French Impressionist composers Claude Debussy and Maurice Ravel, achieved a haunting beauty by improvising on modes and tonal centers instead of chords. He introduced new textures to jazz piano with his romantic, sensitive, introspective style filled with lush harmonies. He found new voicings for the chords,

ichard Davis

becoming the most innovative and influential jazz pianist after Thelonious Monk and Bud Powell, the leading pianists of the bebop revolution. He played notes that suggested the notes of not only the original chords but many other chords, too, so the direction he took was never clearly defined or ordained. He could go in the direction of the root of the original chord of a song, or he could progress to an entirely new chord.

Scott LaFaro, following Evans's lead, became an innovative bassist. In 1961, he made history with Evans on their recordings called *The Village Vanguard Sessions*. LaFaro's work meshed so exquisitely with Evans's and drummer Paul Motian's that they played as if they were one person. Evans and LaFaro sometimes echoed each other's lines, LaFaro playing high on the bass, in its upper register.

Their music could be called the exact opposite of Mingus's. Both Mingus and Evans experimented with harmonies. But Evans had a gentle touch and an understated style. LaFaro kept his strings closer to the fingerboard than most other bebop players placed theirs, so he could be more agile, facile, and virtuosic. The strings were strung so low, however, that he could barely be heard except in recording sessions with proper electronic equipment. The subtlety and beauty of LaFaro's harmonic and rhythmic work with Evans impressed and influenced other bassists—both the older players and the younger ones to come.

Ray Brown met LaFaro on July 4, 1961, backstage at the Newport Jazz Festival in Rhode Island. "He came up to me and introduced himself. I had heard him on records, and I liked the way he played," Brown recalled. "He got his bass and I got mine, and we went into a corner of the tent and must have played for two hours. That man had a lot of talent."[3]

LaFaro died in a car accident later that day. Bill Evans was inconsolable. He stopped playing the piano for a while. When friends urged him to start again, he used a variety of bassists—Chuck Israels, Gary Peacock, Eddie Gomez, and Marc Johnson. Peacock and Gomez were, essentially, offshoots of LaFaro, and went on to establish themselves as masterful leaders.

Gary Peacock: After he started playing the bass while stationed in Germany with the U.S. Army, Peacock performed with some of the best American and European musicians, then went to live in Los Angeles where he worked with a variety of other fine musicians. Settling in New York, he spent a year in Bill Evans's group. His sense of adventure then led him to play with many and varied musicians, some of them experimentalists.

A searcher and a man of many interests, he has lived in Japan, studied Eastern philosophy and science, and gravitated to work with jazz stars who pride themselves on daring to be different. Leading his own groups on albums, Peacock has been praised by many critics, some of whom think he is one of the finest contemporary bassists.

Eddie Gomez, who joined Evans's group in 1966 and stayed until 1977, recorded many albums with Evans, including the highly praised *Intuition* and *Blue in Green*, and two Grammy winners, *At the Montreux Jazz Festival* and Gomez's favorite, *You Must Believe in Spring*, recorded in 1977. That one sounded happier in attitude than Evans was usually noted for. Gomez's sound was haunting, melodic, and above all, horn-like—the sound he has said he most wanted to project. He was able to blend perfectly with Evans; two articulate, smooth musicians, they played spellbinding improvisations.

Gomez, who had admired Milt Hinton and Paul Chambers in particular, had been a bright young bassist in New York before his days with Evans. He won a scholarship for a thousand dollars to the Juilliard School of Music. Well-known jazz musicians hired him. His connections led him to meet Evans and stay in his group for a long time.

Gomez was "scared," he recalled, when he decided to leave Evans. His only plan was to try a variety of experiences. He had learned how to get into and out of a solo and to give and take in dialogues with Evans, among other things. But he felt it was time for him to go on to other jobs for professional growth.

He found fusion, classical, pop recording sessions, bass groups performing Mingus's music, and gigs in acoustic trios whose albums won Grammys. He even played on the percussive pianist McCoy Tyner's record *Supertrios*. "It was very interesting to be around McCoy—a very rhythmic, strong player," Gomez said, "and of course his sound was so different from Evans."[4]

So Gomez built a career as a versatile sideman and then as a group leader and a composer, often writing experimental music. Among his own albums are *Gomez, Discovery, Power Play*, and *Next Future*. For *Power Play* he wrote an exciting, enlivening song called "W. 110th St." It symbolized his enduring love affair with music, which had begun when he lived on that street on Manhattan's Upper West Side as a young immigrant with his family.

He was born in Santurce, Puerto Rico, on October 4, 1944, and he heard the music of the Hispanic culture all around him. But he preferred Miles Davis and even the brothers Tommy and Jimmy Dorsey, who led their own swing-era dance bands. In their music, he said, "I heard how beautiful and lovely the bass was. I heard it sing and flower. That's where the challenges were for me."

He began playing bass when he was twelve. His father, a factory worker, was so impressed that he made a financial sacrifice and bought Eddie a bass. Eddie went to the High School of Music and Art, played in the All-City Orchestra, and performed in a youth band at the Newport Jazz Festival. He learned from good teachers to read charts and to improvise. "And the guys [in school] started calling me Eddie [not Edgardo, his real name] when I began playing music. That may be another reason for my liking music. Here was a kid who desperately wanted to be American, learn the language and be in the mainstream of American life. And all my classmates tended to be gringos. I wanted to be as smart or as much of an idiot as those kids—to fit in." In the end, he fit in every place—in classical, Latin, and mainstream jazz groups, in studio sessions, and on movie soundtracks.

Sam Jones, a Florida-born bassist who played with popular alto saxophonist Cannonball Adderley in the 1950s and 1960s, also set standards for other bassists. In Cannonball's group, Sam played in the rhythm section with drummer Louis Hayes. Together they went to play with Oscar Peterson, one of the most famous and highest-paid pianists in jazz history. Jones replaced Ray Brown in that group. Then he went to play with pianist Cedar Walton and drummer Billy Higgins in another highly regarded trio that toured the world. Other bassists—and musicians on other instruments—loved to listen to Sam. Soulful and bluesy, he could invent the most creative musical passages from basic, simple ideas. In 1981, at age fifty-seven, he died of cancer.

Dozens more truly great modern bassists played rings around the early masters of the instrument. Among the fine newcomers were Cecil McBee, Michael Moore, and Rufus Reid, all of them eventually leaders and composers. Buster Williams, Walter Booker, Andy Simpkins, and others distinguished themselves in vocal and instrumental groups. Buster, Booker, and Simpkins played for singer Sarah Vaughan.

Andy Simpkins also played for eight years, from 1968 to 1976, with pianist George Shearing's popular quintet before joining Vaughan's trio for ten years, from 1979 until shortly before her death in 1990. Simpkins, who also played with other jazz stars, always admired the classic bassists Jimmy Blanton, Milt Hinton, Oscar Pettiford, Ray Brown, Red Mitchell, Charles Mingus, Paul Chambers, and Niels-Henning Orsted Pedersen. These were his influences and heroes. For his entire career, he remained within the mainstream of jazz players.

With Vaughan and others, Simpkins played with symphony orchestras, and he even accompanied the pop superstar Whitney Houston. One of the highlights of his recorded work is the soundtrack of the movie *In Cold Blood*, based on Truman Capote's book. With Ray Brown, Simpkins played the chilling, suspenseful, eerie music to accompany the story of two young pathological killers.

Cecil McBee, who was born in Tulsa, Oklahoma, in 1935, became one of the most versatile players, in part because of his early opportunities to play with very interesting leaders. Arriving in Manhattan with a degree in music education in the mid-1960s, he played with a great saxophonist and composer, Wayne Shorter, at Slug's, a Lower East Side jazz club. Some of the best jazz of the period was performed there.

Jack DeJohnette heard Cecil and recommended him to the idiosyncratic, mysterious saxophonist Charles Lloyd, with whom Cecil then played for about a year. The group played exciting music in Europe and the United States and recorded *Forest Flower* and *Dream Weaver*. One of Cecil's first and most highly regarded compositions, "Song of Her," was included on *Forest Flower*. Cecil thought Lloyd's group was very well balanced creatively and aesthetically. From there, he went on to play with the soulful free jazz saxophonist Pharaoh Sanders in the late 1960s, then with other adventurous group leaders playing a wide variety of styles in the 1970s and 1980s.

Two of Cecil's favorite leaders were Kenny Barron and Joanne Brackeen, among the most highly regarded modern jazz pianists of the late twentieth century. Joanne at times was called controversial because of her percussive, atonal, free jazz compositions. But Cecil said he always felt comfortable performing with her: "I can do anything I want to with Joanne. If I dropped my bass, she would probably say, 'Yeah, that's a nice note,' because she hears music in everything."[5] Joanne loved Cecil's strength, which was required to keep her freewheeling music grounded.

Cecil also taught at the New England Conservatory in Boston and the jazz program at the New School in New York. He continued to perform his compositions in his own groups and as a sideman. "Close to You Alone" is a poignant love song, with a deeply amorous, sighing, flowing bass line. Fleet piano passages in the higher register serve as a perfect foil for the bass lines. That and another song, "Felicite," were recorded on the album *Out There Like This*, with a group called The Leaders. "Felicite" is an Impressionistic triumph that actually sounds like the anguish of a couple breaking up.

More abstract is Cecil's "Portraits," with a melancholy beginning that grows into the sound of distress, intended as a tribute to Mingus—"a master," said Cecil. Mingus went out of his way to show up in audiences when Cecil, at age forty, began leading one of his own groups. Mingus once said he was sick with a cold and asked Cecil to fill in for him with the Mingus group at the Village Vanguard. But then Mingus surprised Cecil by showing up in the audience.

As proof of his versatility, Cecil has also composed a few blues songs. He wrote a very appealing, easily accessible, extended blues called "Sleeping Giant." When he took a group into a trendy Manhattan club in 1994, he scored a hit with the audience with that original blues.

His strongest influences on his playing have been Ray Brown, Oscar Pettiford, Percy Heath, Paul Chambers, and above all Richard Davis: "Davis fabricated new styles, going from group to group. And Paul Chambers had real stable bass lines. I feel that I fit in between Davis and Chambers."

George Mraz came from Czechoslovakia to the United States in 1968, after studying bass at the Prague Conservatory. He enrolled in the Berklee College of Music in Boston, where he concentrated on studying composition and arranging. In the early 1970s, he replaced Sam Jones in pianist Oscar Peterson's group, then joined the Jones-Lewis Orchestra. It became obvious to jazz-loving audiences that Mraz was a great player, with all the qualities of a highly trained classical bassist plus a gift for accompanying and improvising.

In the 1980s, Mraz played peerless accompaniment in the trio of Tommy Flanagan, who established himself as one of the great virtuosos in jazz piano history. Mraz was so highly regarded that when his bass was stolen from a jazz club in the early 1980s, musicians staged a benefit to pay for a new one.

Ron McClure was a particularly fine bassist in leading groups beginning in the 1960s, including Charles Lloyd's band and Blood, Sweat and Tears, a fusion group that become very popular and survived until 1977. He also played with Miles Davis, Sarah Vaughan, and Thelonious Monk. Leaders admired his propulsive rhythmic style.

Scores of other bassists played in many groups. Their numbers were actually startling, because this flowering of fine bassists took place at a time when acoustic jazz itself had gone into commercial eclipse. The bassists, along with most jazz instrumentalists, became part of a lost generation of virtuosos—musicians who played their acoustic instruments at least as well as anyone ever had done, and often better. They were better educated and had inherited a large repertoire and a vast reservoir of techniques. They had earned the freedom to solo more and make themselves prominent in groups. But they had fewer groups, clubs, and concerts to play in. The American public was listening to rock music. If people listened to jazz at all, they usually chose fusion played with electric and acoustic instruments.

The bassists who found a great deal of work began playing the electric instrument with frets—markings on the fingerboard of the bass that show where the notes are. There were unfretted electric basses, too. Jaco Pastorius, the most famous electric bass player, used one. But the majority of young bassists who concentrated on the electric instrument needed the fret markings.

One day, George Duvivier, who worked all the time in the studios in New York, was told to bring an electric bass to a gig. He disliked the instrument so much that he bought an unfretted one. He was gleeful when rock musicians picked it up and became totally lost; without frets, they couldn't figure out where the notes were. Duvivier eventually gave up the electric bass altogether. He didn't have to play it to make a living, so successful had he become as an acoustic musician.

Ray Brown had a similar experience. He never learned to like the electric bass. He, too, had the luxury of refusing to play it, since he was so well established as an acoustic bassist. But he admired young bassists who played the electric instrument well. He liked the talent of *Monk Montgomery*. A brother of guitarist Wes Montgomery, Monk was one of the first jazz bassists to play the electric bass. To soften its sound, he designed a felt pick that was less percussive than the traditional plastic pick. Brown also thought Stanley Clarke, John Patitucci, and Victor Wooten played electric bass exceptionally well. He met them all in the studios on the West Coast; many bassists played jazz and other styles of music primarily in the studios. Though they were not generally known in the jazz world, their accomplishments were admirable.

Some bassists loved both acoustic and electric instruments. That was lucky for them, because in the recording studios, the calls used to go out for acoustic bassists, then for both electric and acoustic bassists, and then for one bassist who could play both instruments. Young musicians were, of course, a product of their own times and accustomed to hearing loud, electric music. Both Robert Hurst and John Patitucci grew up loving both basses. They took offense when other acoustic musicians described the electric bass as a toy or when electric instrumentalists called the acoustic bass a dinosaur.

Rufus Reid also admired both basses. He played acoustic bass first, then electric bass on the side. Eventually he focused on the acoustic instrument, his first love. With that he established himself as a busy jazz player in Chicago. Moving to New York to develop his career, having exhausted the challenges on Chicago's playing scene, he became director of William Patterson College's music department in Wayne, New Jersey. Since the school was close to New York City, he easily maintained his positions as an educator and a revered performer in New York clubs.

He wasn't always enthralled with the music he played for other leaders, so in the 1990s he formed a group called TanaReid, co-led by his friend, drummer Akira Tana. The group played in New York clubs and toured in the United States and abroad. So Rufus had the opportunity to make his dream of playing his original compositions come true. He also led albums such as *Seven Minds*, on which his strong, sure sound provides the foundation for the entire group and emanates, like the spokes of a wheel, throughout its work. Here is a chance to hear a bassist taking complete charge.

Looking back at his career, Rufus, who revered Ray Brown's mastery of the bass, remembered the days in the 1960s when he had moved to Chicago to study and work. Searching for some good music to play, he was hired to do a show that featured pop singing star Liza Minnelli and opera singers. "They had three bass players, not jazz players, and they needed somebody to play electric bass for Liza," Rufus recalled. "When I played the arias [for the opera singers] the other players checked me out to see if I could use the bow, read [music] and follow the conductor. When I played electric bass for Liza, that blew them away. So I became a commodity." He remained in demand for a variety of jobs.[6]

Rufus thought it was unwise for aspiring jazz bassists to limit themselves to straight-ahead, acoustic performances. He counseled them to play both acoustic and electric instruments so that they could expose themselves to a broad spectrum of music and give themselves more employment opportunities. Then they could pay the rent and have enough energy to practice, develop their musicality, broaden their horizons, and play the music they really loved. His own credits have included jobs in Broadway show orchestras and a gig as a substitute electric bass player for the television show *Sesame Street*.

For the most part, the electric and acoustic bass players have lived in separate worlds. The electric players work in rock, pop, and fusion groups. Only a few have crossed over as professionals to play in acoustic jazz groups. Among those who crossed over successfully, winning a place of esteem on both sides of the fence, has been **Bob Cranshaw**. He established himself as an acoustic player. But because of a physical problem, he switched to the electric bass for a long time. Acoustic group leaders continued to hire him because they knew and admired his work so much. Eventually he was able to play acoustic bass again.

Stanley Clarke leads his own groups and composes for movies, playing both acoustic and electric basses. **Robert Hurst** and **John Patitucci** switch back and forth from electric to acoustic instruments. In the 1990s, Hurst could be seen on television, playing both his acoustic and electric basses in the band for the *Tonight* show.

A New York-based woman, **Kim Clarke,** also began crossing back and forth from acoustic to electric basses in the 1980s. There was antifeminist feeling among male jazz musicians. Some were prejudiced against women players, and others simply didn't realize women bassists existed. So Kim had to become accomplished on both basses to take advantage of whatever jobs came up. She played in rock, funk, fusion, and acoustic jazz groups and big bands. The few other women bass players frequently did the same.

It wasn't until the 1990s that a woman playing acoustic bass, *Melissa Slocum,* began getting calls to play regularly with groups led by men and women. Tall and proud, strong and steely-fingered, Melissa possessed all the strengths—excellent time, a highly developed sense of swing, and bright ideas for creative bass lines and solos. When she played with the all-women's big band called Diva, even her bandmates became enthralled by her abilities.

She began playing electric bass in her midwestern hometown. When she arrived in New York City in the early 1980s, she switched to acoustic bass. Her parents gave her money to pay for her graduate school tuition in fine arts. Melissa bought an acoustic bass instead. Her parents took years to calm down about her choice. In the meantime, Melissa became a starving musician.

Then she found a steady job accompanying a woman pianist and singer in a little Greenwich Village club, and she supported herself by keeping that date and running to many other gigs. After a few years, she decided to go back to graduate school, earning master's degrees in jazz bass and then classical bass playing. She wanted to teach for financial security as well as play. She also began to break through the barrier of sexual discrimination in jazz. In addition to all the pressures of her profession, she was also raising a daughter alone by that time.

Jaco Pastorius was regarded as the greatest virtuoso on the electric bass in a variety of styles. He worked occasionally with acoustic jazz musicians and learned a great deal from them. He also studied European classical music from Johann Sebastian Bach to the ultramodernists Paul Hindemith and Igor Stravinsky. But he won fame in fusion groups, particularly Weather Report and his own septet called Word of Mouth.

Born in Pennsylvania and raised in Fort Lauderdale, Florida, Jaco astounded other bassists with his technique and the passion and bril-

𝒥aco Pastorius

liance of his solos. In the 1970s, he was acclaimed as the greatest and most versatile electric bass player in the world.

Ira Sullivan, a saxophonist who worked in a band with young Jaco in 1973, recalled, "When I first met Jaco, he was straight as an arrow and always full of kinetic energy." Pastorius made other people feel inspired and energetic just by being near him and playing with him. "When I knew him, he was a wildcat full of music, but he also had his family together, had his children together, was taking care of business, playing this wonderful music and revolutionizing his instrument."[7]

He began to play and record with Weather Report in 1975. He made two older players in the band, Joe Zawinul and Wayne Shorter, famous composers and players in the jazz world, feel young again. He left to lead his own group. Then the star he was riding began falling to earth. By the early 1980s, he was taking drugs, particularly cocaine, and drinking constantly. He menaced people on and off bandstands.

Hospitalized at times for his problems, he still managed to keep playing very well for several years. Other musicians thought his genius for playing the electric bass was a curse because he could play so well even when he was high. For years, he never had to admit he had drug problems. He traveled around the world to perform for adoring audiences. Other electric bassists in fusion and rhythm-and-blues studied with him and paid him great homage.

Then he began to lose his ability to play. He forgot songs in the middle of performances. Constantly getting into fights, he became too unreliable for anyone to hire him. In September 1987, he was severely beaten by a bouncer at an after-hours club in Fort Lauderdale. Lapsing into a coma, he died about a week later.

Other bassists remembered him as a mad genius who revolutionized the art of electric bass playing with his technique and spirit. In 1995, a book about his life, *Jaco: The Extraordinary and Tragic Life of Jaco Pastorius*, was published by Miller Freeman Books.

The world of the electric bassists is worth a study in itself, with a nearly entirely different pantheon of stars, such as Paul McCartney of the Beatles and Sting. Suffice to say that during the lean days for acoustic jazz in the 1960s and 1970s, it was the heroic, dedicated jazz musician who persisted in following his heart to play any acoustic instrument. The musicians who confined themselves to acoustic groups usually had to struggle to earn meager livings.

Among the acoustic bass players, free jazz players had a particularly difficult time during the reign of rock and fusion jazz. The public virtually ignored their work. They played experimental music in lofts and out-of-the-way clubs. Few people went to hear them. European audiences liked free jazz far more than Americans did. At home, almost all the free jazz players were bona fide starving artists. Even the few who established reputations as interesting musicians had to take odd jobs to support themselves. The most famous free jazz pianist, Cecil Taylor, washed dishes for a while.

Free jazz players used the outer extensions of chords to play on or to improvise from, or no chords at all, just scales and lines. People who were used to listening to the basic three-tone triad—the root, 3rd, and 5th notes of a chord—had difficulty hearing the free music based on the 7th, 9th, 11th, and 13th tones of the chord. Audiences had to grow used to listening to the odd, unsettling, sometimes wild-sounding music. Some became upset by the sound. Solos no longer had to have any chord center, progressions, or form except for what the players made up in their heads. And they certainly didn't follow the twelve-bar blues form or the thirty-two-bar American standard song form.

Some audiences were very critical of the free jazz players and felt they were simply playing a lot of notes. It was as if they were reading words from a dictionary instead of creating good sentences, paragraphs, or stories. In truth, only musicians with a very thorough knowledge of how to play music with established forms could break the rules and perform fascinating free-form music. Many musicians didn't even like free jazz. It required special taste, imagination, and hypersensitivity to the changing, sometimes chaotic society in which artists and everyone else lived.

Charlie Haden and a few other free jazz bassists played in groups with famous but irregularly employed leaders. Among them were saxophonist Ornette Coleman, trumpeter Don Cherry, and pianist Carla

Deep Down in Music

Bley, all very interesting, passionately committed free jazz players. They endured days of financial hardship, artistic neglect, and even public disdain. In the 1960s and 1970s, the free players did nothing to help boost the popularity of acoustic jazz. Their persistent devotion to their own ideas was miraculous because they had only each other to encourage them to keep going.

Some of the free jazz players eventually modified their ideas. Audiences gradually became used to atonal and odd musical sounds, suggestions, and moods. In the 1980s and 1990s, Charlie Haden's reputation grew by leaps and bounds. A widening audience accepted his work. At first, he seemed to have spun his music directly out of the Mingus legacy. But in the 1980s, he was providing fine support for a new jazz piano star, Geri Allen, on her albums of original music with obvious roots in the jazz tradition.

In 1987, Haden formed his Quartet West, playing a wide variety of musical styles—songs made popular in old films, tunes by old jazz players and singers, and his new compositions. He took inspiration from paintings, architecture, and musicians who played in a variety of styles. His taste and talent for lyrical music tempered his flights of free jazz. And his music, now eclectic and all-encompassing, gave him broader appeal.

Fortune began to smile again on the acoustic bassists in the 1970s. *Avery Sharpe* was one of the first young bassists to feel the effect of the public's renewed interest in acoustic jazz. When pianist McCoy Tyner hired Sharpe to go on the road with his group in the 1970s, he was stunned. The commercial state of acoustic jazz had been so gloomy that practical-minded Avery had majored in economics at the University of Massachusetts in Amherst. On the side, because he loved music, he played electric bass, which was in demand for funk bands.

One night, listening to a college radio station, he heard saxophonist John Coltrane playing acoustic jazz. "Overnight I went from Kool & the Gang to Coltrane," he recalled. He began to practice playing acoustic bass. "I thought I couldn't get gigs on acoustic and was wasting my time," he said, "but I loved the sound."[8]

118

By the time he received a master's degree in music and took an administrative job with an insurance company, Avery had developed his acoustic bass playing to a great degree. Saxophonist Archie Shepp, who had been one of Avery's teachers in college, took him on tours. Avery failed to return to his job on schedule from one of his tours in Europe in 1980. He had officially called it a "vacation" to his corporate employers. The company asked him to choose between music and his "day job," as musicians define any job outside of music. Avery had a family to support. He thought he should keep his job. But his wife encouraged him to satisfy his soul. She knew how much he wanted to play music, and she didn't want him to have any regrets.

Drummer Art Blakey asked Avery to join his famed group, the Jazz Messengers, at the same time that McCoy Tyner invited him to go along with his group. Avery went with McCoy. The timing couldn't have been better. At the end of the 1970s, something surprising happened: Jazz started to become trendy.

The Kool Jazz Festival in New York officially recognized jazz's new popularity in 1982 by staging a "Young Lions of Jazz" concert at Carnegie Hall. Avery played in it. So did a young trumpeter named Wynton Marsalis, singer Bobby McFerrin, and other fine young jazz players who had recently distinguished themselves on one instrument or another. The concert was taped and later released as an album.

Sharpe became an acknowledged virtuoso in the renaissance of jazz. Even so, his wife still had to work as a nurse to help pay the bills. Avery's career needed the love and cooperation of his family, and it was worth it for everyone. As a featured sideman in Tyner's trio and big band, Avery attained fame for his technique and creativity. Avery also recorded albums as a group leader. Of course, he aspired to do more work on his own.

10

THE ACOUSTIC JAZZ BASSISTS RISE AGAIN

I n the 1960s and 1970s, it seemed as if nothing would ever drown out the sound of rock. Rhythm-and-blues in the late 1960s had great appeal, too, and served as a handmaiden and musical expression of the aims of the powerful civil rights movement. And everyone danced to disco music, which evolved in the 1970s as a variation of rock.

But pop music started to lose its magnetic hold on the public. The public's taste in popular music keeps changing. The civil rights movement succeeded to a great degree with its public demonstrations, and the fervor for rhythm-and-blues cooled off. Disco music became trendy. Then a video revolution got under way: Teenagers fell in love with anything on a video. Sophisticated college students, postgraduates, and young professionals started looking for a new type of entertainment to fill their leisure hours. Record companies took a chance on reissuing classic jazz albums. The executives were astounded when jazz records started selling.

Columbia Records signed Wynton Marsalis, a brilliant young trumpeter, to a recording contract for jazz and classical music. Everyone bought his albums. His jazz concerts attracted crowds, including young people who had never liked jazz before. In his early twenties, Wynton was on his way to becoming a superstar and a very rich man. He could afford to pay good salaries to his sidemen. And of course wherever Wynton played, a bassist—Reginald Veal, for one—worked behind him, getting his chance to show off.

Other record companies scrambled to find more young Wyntons on all the instruments to sign to record contracts. But record company executives and club owners still resisted the idea of the bass as a lead instrument. The bassists themselves admitted that their acoustic instrument had little innate glamour. A bassist had to have some extra charisma, or spirit, to attract any attention. Young bassist Robert Hurst summed it up, "You can't jump out in the audience and dance around and do all [the things a saxophone can do]. You can't hold a high note forever and get the girls screaming."[1] But some of the new young bassists were strong, creative players with a great deal of drive. Their pizzicato work commanded attention. Audiences loved them. Some young bassists played solos in the upper registers of the instrument so often that they were criticized for neglecting to learn to play the foundation. The controversy simply helped fuel the fire and focus more attention on bassists.

Clubs, concerts, restaurants, recording contracts, and festivals became abundant. And musicians flocked to New York to look for work. *Santi Debriano,* a Panamanian who had grown up in the United States and moved to Paris to play the bass professionally, decided to try his luck in New York. Kirk Lightsey, who was building a reputation as an exciting player in Bradley's, a piano-bass duo room in New York, hired Santi. After that, the jazz world was alerted to the young man's great talents as a supportive player and a soloist. In demand as a sideman, he also began to record albums as a leader of his own group, the Panamaniacs.

Other young musicians heard about the activity in New York and decided to take their chances. Bassist ***Ray Drummond*** was one of them. Ray had always played music on the side of his other pursuits. A college graduate with a master's degree in business, he got bored in boardrooms, and he dropped out of the corporate world to play bass in San Francisco in the 1970s. In 1977, he joined the first wave of the modern musicians' immigration to New York. He played both electric and acoustic basses professionally. He worked so hard, played so well, and had such a knack for socializing with other acoustic musicians that many calls for jobs came to him. In 1979, he played his last job with electric bass and concentrated on the acoustic. He played constantly in New York clubs, on recordings, and in concerts in the United States and other countries. Both as a soloist and a supportive player, he became known as an exciting bassist.

As the 1980s progressed, it seemed as if a promising new bassist with a college degree in music or with conservatory training popped up every week in somebody's group. Art Blakey hired several wonderful bassists, among them Peter Washington, who soon began circulating as a busy freelancer and even followed George Mraz into Tommy Flanagan's trio. Electric bassist Lonnie Plaxico was recognized as a wonderful player, in demand in many groups. David Williams, who had played bass for a long time in Cedar Walton's groups, became so well known that savvy jazz audiences were doubly delighted when he was on any bill. Highly praised by critics, Santi Debriano reacted to the wealth of talent on the scene by returning to school for advanced music degrees. He wanted to be able to teach, too.

Bassists Stafford James, Chris White, Scott Colley, William Parker, Ed Howard, and Ira Coleman became notable sidemen in groups. Dennis Irwin played for the Village Vanguard's Monday night band. Ratzo Harris distinguished himself as a strong player. Charnett Moffett and Christian McBride developed into stars. McBride actually became one of the best-known jazz musicians on any instrument by the 1990s. Leon "Boots" Maleson, who also played classical music, often played double bass in Ron Carter's groups. In 1995, Robert Hurst said he was paying his bills with the acoustic bass. That was how far the fortunes of the acoustic bass had risen during the renaissance of acoustic jazz.

The compact disc gave the jazz renaissance another boost. In the late

1980s, all the record companies began putting their albums out on CD. Everyone was buying the new technology — CD players and new stereos — and then they bought jazz on CDs to replace their old LPs (long-playing records). Some people bought jazz on CD just because they wanted to buy CDs. When they found they really liked it, their enthusiasm made jazz even more popular. People went out to clubs to hear the jazz artists they had learned to like on recordings.

By 1995, it became clear that there were more recording contracts and CDs than clubs for musicians to play in. Some bassists leading their own groups on recordings found it difficult to keep a group together. They couldn't find enough bookings in clubs to make it worthwhile for a group to play together all the time. A leader had to assure sidemen of jobs, or sidemen hopped around from group to group to make a living. The young bass stars who led groups for recordings often played as sidemen in other people's groups. In any case, both as leaders and sidemen, they were gaining experience.

In an article in the *New York Times Magazine* on June 25, 1995, about the recent popularity and musical development of jazz, Milt Hinton was asked who his five favorite bassists were. He listed Ray Brown, Ron Carter, Rufus Reid, Christian McBride, and Lyn Seaton. Christian McBride had one album, *Gettin' to It*, out under his own name as leader by then. As a sideman, he didn't simply enhance groups; his name alone promoted them, and he could draw audiences to clubs and concerts. He was packing a New York club, Iridium, with fans of his group. Charnett Moffett was also striving for individuality as leader of his fusion group, with which he recorded strong-sounding music — a legacy of the 1970s — and starred in Manhattan jazz clubs.

By this time, many jazz musicians had adopted healthy lifestyles. Much of the burden of racial prejudice had lifted, at least from the surface of the lives of African-American players. They lived in middle-class style in integrated communities and went wherever they wanted, whenever they wanted to. Jazz itself was "establishment," commanding respect as a great American art form. The National Endowment for the Arts had begun funding jazz in 1968. Though public funding of the arts was cut in the 1990s, jazz and other art forms were still receiving some government money.

*C*hristian McBride

Once Ray Drummond, for one, established himself as a bassist in demand for other people's groups, he worked hard to find time to lead his own groups. In the late 1980s and 1990s, he gave himself time to write music and organize groups for recordings. Several record companies released his albums. "To me, jazz is about leaping off the precipice," he said to a *Down Beat* magazine writer. "That's part of the lifestyle. We study this music so hard and we live a life which we can adapt to whatever kind of music, whatever kind of mood, whatever kind of feeling, whatever kind of rhythm is asked of us."[2] Ray was talking about the best attitude a musician could have for playing in someone else's group. But he was also expressing his attitude about his responsibility as a leader.

He did find that he had to keep fighting the prejudice against bassists as leaders. It wasn't an easy battle for any bassist to win. Ray won sometimes and led groups in the highly respected Village Vanguard.

The Acoustic Jazz Bassists Rise Again

Bassist Charlie Haden placed high in the music polls for popularity by 1995. Some people thought the albums he led were among the best being released by any instrumentalist. It was a far cry from the days of struggle for this versatile free jazz player.

And young bassists kept arriving in New York City, the place where most jazz musicians felt they ought to prove themselves and seek fame and fortune. There was never a time, not even during the big-band era, when so many musicians chose to play bass and concentrate on acoustic bass. In July 1995, T. S. Monk Jr., a drummer and the son of the famous bebop pianist and composer, was leading his own group at Iridium. He had a new bassist in his lineup: twenty-year-old Gary Wang. T. S. loves to talk as much as his father had liked to stay silent, and he told an audience about Wang's background. Gary had started playing bass as a senior in high school; within a few years, he had become an accomplished artist. "So there's a future for jazz, yes, there's definitely a future for jazz," Monk said.[3] The audience cheered, as another bassist began making his way into the revitalized jazz world.

BASSISTS TALK ABOUT THEIR ART

In this book, we have traced the development of jazz bass against the background of the changing social and musical history of the United States. Many wonderful bassists have not even been mentioned—such diverse players as Bob Cunningham, who played with Dizzy Gillespie, Eric Dolphy, trumpeter Freddie Hubbard, Art Blakey, and many others; Paul West, who directs the music program at the Henry Street Settlement House on New York's Lower East Side; plus Reggie Johnson, Cameron Brown, Gerald Veasley, Fred Hopkins, and many more. It's impossible to include the names of every good bass player. Instead, here are remarks made by a group of bassists about aspects of their art. Their ideas and experiences represent much of what is unique about jazz bassists and what is special about the art of jazz in general.[1]

126

Do you remember when you first started improvising?

Ron Carter: I think jazz players as a general rule have always improvised, if only in the form of rearranging a scale, an exercise, or an étude, to be done differently than it was written. At around the time of my first cello lesson, when I was eleven, I must have picked up the bow and drawn it across the strings and made some sounds that weren't supposed to be made at that point in the lessons. In a sense, that could be defined as improvisation. Most jazz players have always heard this other sound that wasn't being directed at them through a lesson and was more than the lesson offered. And they started to try to find out what else was in there.

Ray Drummond: When I was five years old, I could whistle solos from records. My father used to like to show me off to his friends. I could whistle "Cool and Crazy" from a Shorty Rogers record. I started on trumpet when I was seven, then went to baritone horn. I was consciously aware of trying to improvise in 1960, when I was fourteen and a junior in high school. I led a band with trumpet, not only arranging but trying to get the guys to improvise, even though I didn't have the chops yet.

There are several ways to improvise. By rote: You go get under your fingers a basic, 10,000 phrases, groups of notes, and, as the chords go by, you apply those groupings of notes. Or you play exactly what comes into your brain. You're telling your story. If you have talent, you break away from either method, and you don't know from one second to the next where you're going. And that's the process. I was twenty-five when I decided to be a musician. . . . I knew I would make some kind of contribution; it was only a question of time. The music in me is so strong. That's another great part of the improvisational process.

George Duvivier: I was a classical violinist. I switched to classical bass in 1938 and did some of my first improvisation that year, imitating Slam Stewart. And I recall when "Big Noise from Winnetka" came out. Ray Bauduc, the drummer, who came out of Bob Crosby's Bobcats, (a swing-era band) would lean over with his sticks and play on the bass, while the bassist fingered the strings. It was the first time I ever saw that done. I did it, too, by putting my fingers across the strings: ding-a-ding-a-ding. (Later on he found out that it had taken two men, a bassist and drummer, to get the sound that he learned to do alone.) Then I joined Coleman Hawkins at Kelly's Stable in Manhattan and started improvisation. He forced me to, gave me introductions to play in every conceivable key, for example a blues in G flat! I learned so much that I worked with Billie Holiday and a very young Helen Humes (a jazz singer who began her professional career with Count Basie's band.) A pianist-arranger Clyde Hart helped me with the bass line, the concept of playing, to make a better choice of notes. He showed me transitional notes, prettier stuff. I called it "Four Months at Hawkins University."

Michael Moore: I began improvising on the piano by ear at age six or seven, entertaining myself with melodies. I played "When Johnny Comes Marching Home Again" in a minor key and thought that seemed really great. At age fifteen, I started playing bass with my father, a guitarist. He would teach me chord changes. I would improvise from there. My father understood harmony well, but he didn't know how to teach improvisation. He played by ear. Through trial and error, I got better and eventually met sophisticated players who also taught techniques. By the time I was eighteen in Cincinnati, I studied classical music, piano lessons, in 1965, and learned more about harmony. I've found keyboard harmony study to be really important for improvisation.

Brian Torff: I would take some thing from the radio, a chord from a Beatles song, or a tune, and try to play it on the piano. That's the way to begin. You hear a sound, you find what it is: then you find your way of playing it.

What Did You Do To Acquire Skills To Improvise?

Ron Carter: Just sitting down and figuring out how does this chord work in relation to the next chord. What notes are in this chord? Why does this chord sound that way? If I change this note in this chord, how does that affect the sound of the chord? Once you start to get involved in this kind of theoretical expression, you see if this expression on paper works on an instrument. You go through trial and error with theory on paper and make the alterations on the instrument to try to understand why something doesn't work and how it can be made to work. You listen a lot. You listen to Charlie Parker, for example: how was he able to make this B flat seven chord sound that way when someone else can't get that kind of sound out of it? Or you listen to Miles Davis; say the chord is spelled FACEflat. What makes his B natural sound correct? You backtrack and find out that four measures before, he made this figure that now translates into this note B natural. So you get very analytical. A lot of thought goes into determining what ideas work.

When a bass player plays a bass line, he uses the same improvisation on the scales as a saxophone player playing a solo; the bassist does it much more often, for the whole length of the tune, while the saxophone player plays a solo and sits down. The bass player is still improvising with these same chords. So in a sense, it's much more difficult to build a bass line because the bass player has to do it so much more.

Ray Drummond: I listened to others with an ear to duplicate, if not the exact notes, then the feelings or the problems that they're solving—the problems of tension and release, and whether the music is humorous or sad or spiritual. People get the feeling. If you're clumsy, people might say you're honest, truthful, but awkward with your language. Some musicians have clarity, some are awkward. There aren't many people as lucid as Charlie Parker or Sonny Rollins.

And I listened to Chet Baker, Shorty Rogers, Paul Desmond, Miles Davis, Sarah Vaughan, Count Basie, Eartha Kitt. I've . . . gotten into the vocalists and their lyrics. . . . It has become important for me with a ballad to speak those words through the instrument. A lot of old musicians tell you to know the lyrics; guided by that, you can improvise off the music. Ultimately what you're doing is mimicking the human voice. So I've realized I want to tell stories musically. I ask myself: How do I become a perfect conduit? What are my strengths and weaknesses: You look for the musicians closest to you in spirit. It's a process of doing research. You hear a phrase by Bird that you dig. So you write it down, play it, analyze it. You unlock it and integrate it. That's the essence of what I do. It's a process that will never die. You're no longer imitating phrases. And your facility with your instrument becomes so great that you're playing your own personality.

George Duvivier: I started the violin at age eight and played in the Central Manhattan Symphony. I loved music, didn't mind practicing, and switched to the bass because of the work opportunities in those days. All along, every fifteen minutes on the radio, there was a different band. I was exposed to every conceivable type of music, all the way up to Jimmy Lunceford and Duke Ellington . . . their sounds, arrangements, musical disciplines. When I switched to the bass, I worked like the devil. The bass represented a reversal of strings, a different clef, and intervals tremendously extended over the violin's. In that era, around 1938, there weren't many bass soloists. I listened to horn players and guitarists: Hawkins, Chu Berry, Ben Webster, Roy Eldridge, the beautiful, melodious Bunny Berigan, Armstrong, and Charlie Christian, who influenced the playing of so many instrumentalists. If you listen to Oscar Pettiford, particularly after he switched to cello in his later years, the lines he plays are from [guitarist] Charlie Christian. And I like to think of Christian a lot even today when I'm playing. It's foot patting music; it just swings.

Michael Moore: When I was with my father, we used to sing certain things, as we drove along in the car—like Nat King Cole's "Straighten Up and Fly Right." I was able to phrase properly rhythmically, singing from an early age, even though I couldn't play yet. And I use that as a guide for my students now. If they can sing it rhythmically correct, swing it, then they can have the potential to play jazz. If they can't do that, they have a serious problem. So sing an Armstrong or a Lester Young solo and phrase it the way they do.

Also I may take a blues and make my students play a whole tune on one note to see how much rhythmic variety they can develop. Sonny Rollins can play something on one note and have them jumping up and down in the aisles. That points up to young players what they're supposed to be doing, playing interesting and swinging rhythms.

George Mraz: When I first came to the States in 1968, I went to Berklee College of Music for three semesters. In harmony classes, they asked me to write a few lines as if we were playing them. I think we had to sing them, too. That's a good idea. If you can't sing it, you can't play it. And if it's in your head, somehow your fingers will get you there.

It's important to learn ear training for improvisation. You start with hearing intervals, then go on to sequences of intervals and phrases and be able to sing them. And learn to transpose a simple idea to all keys. If you learn a new tune, try to play it in three or four different keys, or ideally all 12, so that you can retain it better.

Brian Torff: I took a Wynton Kelly [piano] solo and wrote it out. It took me months. Then I played it on the bass. As a result of going through the whole process, I had my own approach. The process clues me into phrasing and opens up new doors for me. I find that as a bass player, you learn the fundamentals of your instrument, with good rhythm and a good sense of time to supply the bottom to groups. And then for soloists it's another ball game. I listened to bassists having trouble making the transition from background to lead player. So I decided that I'm just going to listen to horn players and singers, people who lead all the time. And I'll forget that I'm a bass player. I'm just a musician. That freed me. I worked hard to get a natural flow through the instrument, so I don't think: it's a bass, it's big.

What Do You Look for In a Partner To Play Improvisation With?

Ron Carter: I look for sensitivity to my direction, musicians' abilities to assist me, their trusting me that I really mean this note B natural on this F seventh chord. And if they follow my trend of thought, they'll see that things work out right down the line. I look for their improvisation of the scales to see how they make this note work—why does it work so well for one in this measure and not for me in the same measure four choruses later?

I look for their sense of the chords: how they use the chords, how they voice a chord, where they play a chord, where they don't play a chord. I look for their ability to get as much tonal qualities out of an instrument as are available to them, and not to get locked into a sound.

I look for the inquisitive mind: people who want to sit down and discuss what they did the night before; who discuss what doesn't work for them and how you can help them figure out why something works; who discuss their experiences, successes and failures. People who are adventurous can satisfy my need. I'm not a safe player. . . . I play with anyone who is aggressive and adventurous. And this is what I call jazz.

Ray Drummond: I look for someone whom I can listen to, and who trades, as in the ideal male-female relationship. . . . My favorite improvisational partners are guys with a sense of harmony, or a rhythmic thing, or improvisational talents. I hope for the space to grow. I feel it's the ultimate compliment when something greater than either of us comes out of us. That's not improvisation. That's music.

George Duvivier: I look for someone who will listen, listen, listen. That's hard to come by.

Brian Torff: I look for rapport, as you do in a good friend. Someone who likes you. When you talk, he listens and vice versa. You hope you inspire each other. If one has a down day, the other might light a fire.

Do You Get Into Improvisational Ruts and, If So, What Do You Do To Get Out?

Ron Carter: It seems to me that jazz players have been saddled with the obligation and responsibility that they cannot play the same thing twice. If they do, they must be in a rut. What gives the critic a right to question repetition? If I use the same phrase once in the first set and again in the second set, am I in an improvisational rut? No. I'm always trying to get to another level, to play better than I played last night or last set. It's a measure of my growth to see if I'm more consistent, more even in my tone quality, or with my intensity of phrases, in picking the right notes to play. If it means that I'm going to play the same phrase every night, I'm comfortable to do that.

Ray Drummond: I get into ruts, and then begin to learn some new tunes, and include them in my practice, improvise off them; they create new ruts, destroying the old ruts. And you move on to the next rut. Change, yeah, keep changing.

Michael Moore: Sometimes I get tired of hearing myself. It's like . . . a slump in baseball. You start to change your batting style, your foot position, your bat, your shirt, and usually it all gets worse. The thing is not to think about the problem. Try to get to work each night, play what you're thinking about. Don't dwell. The more you think about it, the worse it gets.

Brian Torff: Usually it means that you've been playing the same material too long with the same people.

Does the Bass Have Improvisational Limitations?

Ron Carter: The bass is big, the intervals are far apart. If one could find a way to circumvent that, the bass would present fewer problems in improvisation. There are no frets, no keys, no marks to show you where the notes are. The bass player has only an unmarked fingerboard that's forty to forty-two inches long. But there have been great players who have taken this cumbersome length and made it do something different and gone from one stage to another. I want to be one of those guys who have done something different with the bass, even with its limitations . . . and to conquer the big intervals.

Ray Drummond: Sometimes it's physically impossible to play a passage in tune. Only the string instruments have this pitch problem, but we have to play in tune. And it's a lifelong pursuit. With an unfretted instrument, the note is there, but you have to get it. So the bass is very different from other instruments. It's very hard to play this monster.

Michael Moore: Every instrument has a language of its own. You learn to say things one way on one instrument. Some things that happen on piano never do on bass. Get your language down and speak in that language.

Know what your own language can do. Each bassist also has his own limitations. [Pianist Thelonious] Monk played his way because he was limited, and through that limitation found his own complete language and his directions. Some guys have no limitations and consequently no style. Even too much talent is detrimental to style and individuality. Van Gogh couldn't paint like Michelangelo but could do what he did. There's one built-in limitation: bass players are always playing the root of the chord up. So I devised a method to get away from that for solos. I think from the top down.

George Duvivier: The size of the bass no longer limits the solo potential of the instrument, as each succeeding generation since the 1930s has built speed—from the slap bass days, when practitioners weren't too skilled with left hand fingering—to the pizzicato style of Blanton—right up through the pizzicato done with the second, third, and fourth fingers of the right hand, in the style of playing a concert guitar, if you will. And toward that end, many soloists are playing from the mid-range of the instrument upward for the solos, because the intervals are close. And probably in the next ten years, someone will come along and play "Flight of the Bumble Bee" pizzicato on bass—that is, if someone hasn't already done so.

Source Notes

Chapter One

1   Pat Cole, "Defending the Bottom Line," *Down Beat* magazine (April 1995), p. 29.
2   Cecil McBee has supplied technical information about the structure of the bass, playing techniques, and the quality of amplification for this chapter and throughout the book.

Chapter Two

1   *Pops Foster: the Autobiography of a New Orleans Jazzman*, as told to Tom Stoddard (University of California Press, Berkeley, California, 1971), p. 76.
2   Ibid, p. 4.
3   Ibid, p. 14.
4   Ibid, p. 18.
5   Ibid.
6   Ibid, p. 19.
7   Ibid, Introduction, p. xii.
8   Ibid, p. 76.
9   Ibid, Introduction, p. xviii.
10   Ibid, Introduction, p. xvi.
11   Ibid., Introduction, p. xxii.
12   Rex Stewart, *Jazz Masters of the '30s* (Macmillan, New York, 1972, and Da Capo, New York, 1985), p. 11 of Da Capo edition.
13   Ibid., p. 18.
14   Leslie Gourse, *Louis' Children* (William Morrow & Co., New York, 1984), p. 151.
15   *The New Grove Dictionary of Jazz*, edited by Barry Kernfeld (St. Martin's Press, 1995), p. 146.

Chapter Three

1   Edward Kennedy Ellington, *Music Is My Mistress* (Da Capo, New York, 1980), p. 164.
2   Ibid.
3   Ibid.
4   Ira Gitler, *Swing to Bop* (Oxford University Press, New York, 1985), p. 44.
5   Ibid., p. 45.
6   Ibid., pp. 44–45.
7   Ira Gitler, *Jazz Masters of the '40s* (Da Capo, New York, 1984), p. 152.

Chapter Four

1   Kyle Hernandez, *An Introduction to Jazz Bassists*, entry on "Milt Hinton," a doctoral degree paper done for Professor Richard Davis at the University of Wisconsin, unpublished, Madison, Wisconsin, 1995.
2   Milt Hinton and David Berger, *Bass Line* (Temple University Press, Philadelphia, Pennsylvania, 1988), p. 10.
3   Ibid., pp. 24–25.
4   Ibid., p. 29.
5   Ibid., p. 32.
6   Ibid., p. 33.
7   Ibid., p. 51.
8   Ibid.
9   Ibid, p. 90.

Chapter Five

1   Leslie Gourse, "Slam Stewart: He Gave the Bass a Voice," *Frets* magazine (November 1983), pp. 30–31.
2   Edward Berger, *Bassically Speaking, an Oral History of George Duvivier* (Institute of Jazz Studies, Rutgers University, and Scarecrow Press, Metuchen, New Jersey, and London, 1993), p. 135.
3   Gourse, "Slam Stewart," pp. 30–31.
4   Ibid.
5   Leslie Gourse, "Major Holley, Carrying It On," *Frets* magazine (November 1983), p. 31. Subsequent quotations of Major Holley are from this source.

Chapter Six

1   Ira Gitler, *Jazz Masters of the '40s* (Da Capo, New York, 1984), p. 154.
2   Ibid.
3   Ibid., p. 153.
4   Ibid., p. 155.
5   Ibid., p. 145.
6   Ibid., p. 156.
7   Ibid., p. 157.
8   Ibid., p. 162.
9   Ibid., p. 170.
10   Dizzy Gillespie and Al Fraser, *To Be or Not To Bop* (Doubleday, Garden City, and Da Capo, New York, 1979), p. 242 of Da Capo edition.

11   Richard Johnston, "Ray Brown," *Bass Player* magazine (1993), p. 46.

Chapter Seven
1   Zann Stewart, liner notes for *Walkin' the Basses*, an album led by Leroy Vinnegar, Contemporary label, 1993.
2   Ibid.
3   Red Callender and Elaine Cohen, *Unfinished Dream* (Quartet Books, London, 1985), p. 5.
4   Ibid., p. 9.
5   Ibid., p. 10.
6   Ibid., p. 11.
7   Ibid., p. 16.
8   Ibid.
9   Ibid., pp. 20–21.
10   Ibid., p. 24.
11   Ibid., p. 36.
12   Ibid., p. 46.
13   All material comes from the author's interviews with Red Mitchell in New York in the 1980s, with the exception of the information about Red Mitchell's influence in the recording studios. That information comes from a personal interview with Rufus Reid, the jazz educator and bassist profiled in this book.

Chapter Eight
1   Charles Mingus with Nel King, *Beneath the Underdog* (Penguin Books, New York, 1981), p. 12.
2   Ibid, p. 56.
3   Ibid, pp. 38–39.
4   Ibid.
5   Edward Kennedy Ellington, *Music Is My Mistress* (Da Capo, New York, 1980), pp. 293–294.
6   Bill Milkowski, "Charles Mingus—Still Among Us," *Jazz Times* (April 1994), p. 33.
7   Charles Mingus, liner notes for *Let My Children Hear Music*, Columbia/Legacy label, 1971 (reissued 1992).

8   The major New York jazz festival was first called Newport, then changed to the Kool Jazz Festival, and then the JVC Jazz Festival.
9   From an interview by author with Rufus Reid.

Chapter Nine
1   Interview by author with pianist Roberta Piket, 1995.
2   Interview by author with Richard Davis, 1995.
3   Richard Johnston, "Ray Brown," *Bass Player* magazine (March 1993), p. 44.
4   Leslie Gourse, "The Importance of Being Eddie Gomez," *Jazz Times* (June 1988), p. 17. Subsequent quotations of Gomez are from this source.
5   Leslie Gourse, "Cecil McBee," *Jazz Times* (March 1989), p. 31. Subsequent quotations of McBee are from this source.
6   Leslie Gourse, "Surviving as a Jazz Bassist," *Bass Player* magazine (March 1993), pp. 14–15.
7   Bill Milkowski, "Jaco Pastorius, Man & Myth," *Jazz Times* (April 1993), p. 24.
8   Gourse, "Surviving as a Jazz Bassist," pp. 14-15.

Chapter Ten
1   "Defending the Bottom Line," edited by Pat Cole, *Down Beat* magazine (April 1995), p. 29.
2   Mitchell Seidel, "The Conversation," *Down Beat* magazine (March 1993), p. 26.
3   Interview by author with Thelonious Monk III.

Appendix
1   Material for appendix from Leslie Gourse, "The Roundtable," *Jazz Educators Journal*, International Association of Jazz Educators (Fall, 1990), pp. 66–71.

Suggested Listening

In many cases, recommended compact discs are led by musicians other than the bassists, who distinguished themselves as sidemen and became very well known for enhancing the groups they played in. Some CDs are led by bassists. Their work chosen for this list is a mere sampling of their achievements. Where no date is given for the release or reissue date, none is known.

The Early, Slap Bassists

The first bassists almost never led their own groups, but they did play in highly respected groups. In well-stocked music stores, search the bins for recordings led by:

Johnny Dodds, clarinetist, for a sampling of bassist **Bill Johnson**.

Jean Goldkette, big-band leader, for a sampling of bassist **Steve Brown**.

Louis Armstrong, trumpeter, for a sampling of the best-known slap bassist, **George Murphy "Pops" Foster**.

The Big-Band Era Bassists

Jimmy Blanton:
> *Duke Ellington: The Blanton-Webster Band*, recorded from December 1940 to December 1941, RCA, 1986.

Milt Hinton:
> *Cab Calloway and His Orchestra*, 1941-1942, Classics Recordings, 1993.
> *Back to Bass-ics*, Progressive label.
> *Laughing at Life*, Columbia, 1995.
> *Old Man Time*, Chiaroscuro, 1990.
> Also, a collection called *The Modern Art of Jazz*, Biograph Records, 1991, has recordings by both Milt Hinton and Oscar Pettiford.

Slam Stewart:
> *Slim and Slam Complete Recordings*, 1938-1942, Affinity label.
> *Slam Stewart*, Black and Blue, 1972.
> *Two Big Mice* and *Shut Yo' Mouth*, with bassist **Major Holley**, Black and Blue.

Leroy Vinnegar:
> *Leroy Walks Again*, Original Jazz Classics, 1962.

> *Walkin' the Basses*, Contemporary Records, 1993.

Bebop-Era Bassists

These bassists began playing at the end of the swing era and played in early bebop-era groups led by such pioneers as Dizzy Gillespie and Thelonious Monk. Their careers spanned and encompassed all the eras of jazz.

Oscar Pettiford:
> Oscar Pettiford Orchestra, *Deep Passion*, GRP.
> Oscar Pettiford, *Montmartre Blues*, Black Lion, 1990.
> Also, *The Modern Art of Jazz*—See Milt Hinton listing.

Ray Brown:
> *The Oscar Peterson Trio at the Stratford Shakespearean Festival*, Verve, 1956.
> *Seven Steps to Heaven*, Telarc, 1995.

Red Callender:
> Red Callender Combo on a compilation, *The Swing Time Record Story*, Capricorn.

Red Mitchell:
> *Presenting Red Mitchell*, Original Jazz Classics, 1958.
> *Two of a Mind*, with Bill Mays, ITT.

Modern Bassists

Ron Carter:
> *Seven Steps to Heaven*, led by Miles Davis, Legacy, 1992.
> *Telephone*, with guitarist Jim Hall, Concord, 1985.
> *Standard Bearer*, recorded 1972-1979, Milestone, released in 1988.
> (Carter played on many classic Miles Davis albums in the 1960s and has led and played in countless groups since.)

Richard Davis:
> *Live at Sweet Basil*, Evidence, 1994.

Scott LaFaro:
> *Sunday at the Village Vanguard*, with leader Bill Evans, pianist, and Paul Motian, drummer, Riverside, 1987.

Eddie Gomez:
> *Gomez*, Denon, 1984.
> *Live in Moscow*, B&W Music, 1992.

Paul Chambers:
> *Milestones*, led by Miles Davis, Columbia, 1958.

Niels-Henning Orsted Pedersen:
Scandinavian Wood, Caprice, 1996.
Hommage, Emarcy, 1993.
Also many albums led by Oscar Peterson, pianist.

Charles Mingus:
Epitaph, Columbia, 1990.
Fables of Faubus, Four Star, 1993.
Good Bye Pork Pie Hat, Eclipse Records, 1997.

Charlie Haden:
The Shape of Jazz to Come, led by saxophonist Ornette Coleman, Atlantic, 1959. (Reissued on Rhino Records.)
Quartet West, Verve, 1986.
Beyond the Missouri Sky, with Pat Metheny, Verve, 1997.

Rufus Reid:
Perpetual Stroll, Sunnyside, 1980.
Seven Minds, Sunnyside, 1984.
TanaReid, Concord, 1991.

Cecil McBee:
Alternate Spaces, India Navigation, 1996.
McBee has played on countless albums as a sideman, including CDs led by pianist Joanne Brackeen and a cooperative group called The Leaders.

Ray Drummond:
One to One, with Bill Mays, DMP, 1990.
Two of a Kind, with John Hicks, Evidence, 1989.
As leader: *Excursion*, Arabesque, 1993, and *Camera in a Bag*, Criss Cross.

George Mraz:
My Foolish Heart, Milestone, 1996.
Jazz, Milestone, 1996.
Mraz also played as a sideman in pianist Tommy Flanagan's group for many years, for which there are many recordings.

Michael Moore:
With pianist Bill Charlap, on Concord Duo series, 1995.

With Gene Bertoncini, guitarist, on *Art of the Duo*, Stash.
Jobim: Someone To Light Up My Life, Chiaroscuro, 1997.

Dave Holland:
Life Cycle, ECM, 1982.
Triplicate, ECM, 1988.
Dave Holland Quartet, *Dream of the Elders*, ECM, 1996.
Holland has played on many albums as a sideman, including Miles Davis recordings beginning in the late 1960s.

Avery Sharpe:
Sharpe plays with pianist McCoy Tyner's group.
Unspoken Words, Sunnyside, 1988, is his debut as a leader.

Santi Debriano:
Obeah, Freelance.

Christian McBride:
Gettin' to It, Verve, 1995.
Number Two Express, Verve, 1996.

Peter Washington:
This young contemporary sideman now plays in pianist Tommy Flanagan's group.

Electric Bassists

Monk Montgomery:
It's Never Too Late, Mo Jazz, 1970.

Jaco Pastorius:
Jaco Pastorius, CBS Epic, 1976.
Jaco, IAI, 1974.
With Weather Report, *Heavy Weather*, Columbia, 1977.

Steve Swallow:
Swallow crosses back and forth to play both electric and acoustic basses.
Duets, with Carla Bley, ECM/Watt, 1988.
Go Together, Watt, 1993.
Songs With Legs, Watt, 1994.
Carla Bley Big Band Theory, Watt, 1993.

For More Information

The music magazines have published many excellent articles about classic and contemporary jazz bassists. Many libraries keep back issues, and current issues are for sale on newsstands. Among the magazines generally available are *Down Beat*, *Jazz Times*, *Jazz Iz*, and *Bass Player*.

Berger, Edward. *Bassically Speaking, an Oral History of George Duvivier*. Institute of Jazz Studies, Rutgers University. Metuchen, N.J.: Scarecrow Press, 1993.

Callender, Red, and Elaine Cohen. *Unfinished Dream*. London: Quartet Books, 1985.

Foster, Pops, as told to Tom Stoddard. *The Autobiography of Pops Foster*. Berkeley: University of California Press, 1971.

Gitler, Ira. *Jazz Masters of the '40s*. New York: Da Capo, 1984.

Hinton, Milt, and David Berger. *Bass Line*. Philadelphia, Pa.: Temple University Press, 1988.

Milkowski, Bill. *Jaco: The Extraordinary and Tragic Life of Jaco Pastorius*. San Francisco: Miller Freeman Books, 1995.

Mingus, Charles. *Let My Children Hear Music*. Liner notes. Collected in *Setting the Tempo: Fifty Years of Great Jazz Liner Notes*, edited by Tom Piazza (Anchor Books, New York, 1996).

Mingus, Charles, with Nel King. *Beneath the Underdog*. New York: Penguin Books, 1981.

Priestley, Brian. *Mingus: A Critical Biography*. New York: Da Capo, 1982.

Ruff, Willie. *A Call to Assembly*. New York: Viking Press, 1991.

Technical Books on Jazz Bass

Carter, Ron. *Charlie Parker*. Transcribed bass lines to the chord changes of standard bebop songs. Volume 6 of Bass Lines. $5.95.

Coolman, Todd. *The Bottom Line*. The bass line construction, sound production, practicing, special effects, blues/rhythm, slow/fast tempos, and time/feel. Each chapter has review exercises for acoustic or electric bassists. $9.95.

Coolman, Todd. *The Bass Tradition*. Biographies, discographies, and transcribed solos with commentary. $9.95. (Other bassists have great respect for books by Coolman, himself a wonderful Bass Player.)

Cranshaw, Bob. *Blues in All Keys*. Transcribed bass lines for a study of the blues walking bass. Volume 42 of Bass Lines. $4.95.

Goldsby, John. *Bowing Techniques for the Improvising Bassist*. Step-by-step instruction and transcriptions of acoustic bass masters, written by a highly respected jazz bassist. $11.95.

Reid, Rufus. *The Evolving Bassist*. For symphonic and jazz bassists, $17.00. Also, *Evolving Upward—Bass Book 2*. For developing thumb position and expanded bass line and solo techniques. $7.95.

Detailed transcriptions of music played by bassists such as John Patitucci and Jaco Pastorius have been published by Jamey Aebersold Jazz Incorporated, P.O. Box 1244, New Albany, IN 47150 (phone 800-456-1388).

Other books on techniques are available from Miller Freeman books, 6600 Silacci Way, Gilroy, CA 95020 (phone 800-848-5594). Bookstores and music stores often carry technique books, too.

Out of print but possibly in your library: Brown, Ray. *Bass Method*. Mail Box Music. Davis, Richard. *Walking on Chords*. RR&R Music Publishers.

Internet Sites

Due to the changeable nature of the Internet, sites appear and disappear very quickly. Internet addresses must be entered exactly as they appear:

The Internet contains a mindboggling amount of information about jazz; the innumerable Web sites contain information about artists, groups, styles and eras of jazz, record labels, recordings, festivals, concert dates, radio stations, and more. It's perhaps easiest to start with sites that consist primarily of links to other resources. A couple of superior examples:

The Jazz Web, maintained by radio station WNUR-FM at Northwestern University in Evanston, Illinois:
http://www.acns.nwu.edu/WNUR/jazz/

and a site called the Contemporary List of JAZZ Links:
http://www.pk.edu.pl/~pmj/jazzlinks/

The International Society of Bassists does great work to develop a community of people who play the instrument in all genres. The Web site contains forums for people with particular interests:
http://www.jmu.edu/bassists/isb.html

Many performers maintain their own home pages as well, where you can find biographical information, current projects, tour dates, and much more. Among the bass players with home pages:

Rufus Reid:
http://www.jazzcorner.com/reidhome.html

Dave Holland:
http://www.citw.com/holland/index.html

Charlie Haden:
http://interjazz.com/haden/index.html

There's even The Real Mingus Web, all about the life, music, and legacy of Charles Mingus as well as the ongoing work of the Mingus Big Band:
http://www.mingusmingusmingus.com/

Index

Page numbers in *italics* refer to photographs. Principal references to musicians appear in **boldface**.